GW00646844

East Devon Golf Club

Centenary History
1902 – 2002

Kathleen Harland

First published 2001 by Southgate Publishers Ltd for and on behalf of the East Devon Golf Club.

Southgate Publishers Ltd, The Square, Sandford, Crediton, Devon EX17 4LW.

Printed and bound in Great Britain by Short Run Press Ltd, Devon.

British Library Cataloguing in Publication Data
A CIP catalogue record for this book is available from the British Library.

ISBN: 1–85741–084–X

Preface

BY THE RT. HON. LORD CLINTON

As President of the East Devon Golf Club, I am delighted to be able to record a few words in the Centenary Book which marks the first one hundred years in the history of the club and I am honoured to be the President at this unique moment in the club's development, for two reasons. Firstly, my predecessors played a very important part in its formation, and secondly, the membership subsequently over the years have created an outstanding golf club in Budleigh of which we can all be justly proud.

Sir Henry Rolle first came to Devon at the beginning of the sixteenth century so my family have had strong connections with the county for almost five hundred years. The family became interested in the development of Budleigh Salterton when the present Bicton house and gardens were created towards the end of the eighteenth century, but it was the Hon. Mark George Kerr Trefusis, second son of Lord Clinton, who later assumed the name Rolle, who was involved in the formation of the club. You will read more about this in the pages which follow.

Since its inception there have been a great number of improvements to both course and clubhouse, culminating in the present structure and layout. It is a fitting memorial to the early pioneers and to all those who have been involved in the club from its beginnings to the present day.

They are to be congratulated on producing a golf course which is so highly rated throughout the South West and which demands the full concentration of those who play it because of the stunning views. The family are delighted to have been able to provide the means and I wish the East Devon Golf Club continued success in the next one hundred years.

Contents

Acknowledgements

A great number of people have been involved in the publication of this book and the preparations for the centenary year. My task is now formally to thank them and I apologise if I inadvertently forget to mention anyone, since so many people have contributed in one way or another.

Work on the book began long before I was appointed to form, and chair, a Centenary Committee in 1997. Tony Sage and Brian Smith had started researching the history of East Devon Golf Club and had collected a considerable amount of material before Kathleen Harland, the author, became involved. It provided a good basis from which to work but a lot more was needed. With her academic background Kathleen spent over 1000 hours piecing together additional facts from the records at Clinton Devon Estates' offices in East Budleigh, and from other sources, to write what I think is a most interesting and illuminating history of our first 100 years. I cannot thank her enough for what she has done and the club is deeply indebted to her for carrying out this mammoth task.

Of the other people who have played a part I would also like to give a special mention to Brian Smith. With his interest in golfing history and golfing memorabilia Brian has collected some amazing old photographs of the course and clubhouse from the early years and the illustrations in the book, together with details of the early course layout, are mostly a result of his efforts.

Thanks are also due to Thelma Philp, Sue Burley, Pam Roberts, Jane Leggott and the Secretary, Bob Burley, for undertaking the typing and putting it on to disk. It was a time-consuming job. I would especially like to thank Lord Clinton for producing some personal material and for allowing us access to the estate's records, and also Gerald Millington, the estate's archivist, for his assistance.

I would also like to record the Club's sincere thanks to Lord Clinton for his generous presentation of "The Clinton Centenary Vase," to be played for annually, which will take pride of place in our clubhouse.

The Ladies Section was originally researched by Dorothy Oag, with Hilary Greenaway producing the county honours list, and I thank them. Many members produced anecdotes from their personal recollections and submitted photographs and thanks are due to them for their interest, particularly Bill Peaker, Bill Clarke, Norman Richards, Dr David Evans and Dr A. G. Scott Langley, the grandson of our first captain.

The Centenary Committee dealt with the business side of production and Jeremy Price and I joined Tony, Brian and Kathleen to help with the editing. I would like to thank them all for the many hours the team spent pouring over the manuscript and photographs. I would also like to praise Ken Barrett for the magnificent photographs he has taken of the course. Apart from those that appear in the book, many will be retained, in an album, as a photographic record of all 18 holes for posterity.

I have reserved a special thank you to the Centenary Committee until last. Early members were John Jones, Malcolm Baker and Jean Benzie, until their places were taken by Jeremy Price and the two Centenary Captains, Jill Miller and Roy Greenaway. The longest-serving members, with me, were David Watson (Chairman of the Management Committee) and Brian Smith. David has been tirelessly enthusiastic, despite his other commitments, and long-suffering at the hands of some of the suppliers he has had to deal with! However, he has borne these trials and tribulations with his usual good humour and I am indebted to him.

I must also thank Graeme Baxter, the world's foremost golf course artist, for agreeing to accept a commission on behalf of the Centenary Committee to paint a picture of our course. Graeme, despite being in only his 44th year, has already achieved notoriety in that he is the official artist for the Ryder Cup, the Open Championship and the Presidents Cup.

He is also appointed by the P.G.A. and the European Tour but has still managed to make East Devon one of the eight commissions he accepts each year. We will therefore be joining the ranks of Wentworth, Muirfield and Sunningdale who also have Baxter paintings hanging on their clubhouse walls. I am also indebted to the three members who underwrote the project and to the members who have subscribed to the limited edition print.

The Centenary Committee would also like to thank the Management and Captains' Committees for their input into this event. These committees have had the responsibility of presenting the course and clubhouse in keeping with our new status as a centenarian club and organising the competitions.

I hope everyone will enjoy reading the book and joining in the events of the centenary year as they unfold. It has been an honour, a pleasure and a privilege to serve the golf club in this capacity. I doubt I will be called upon to do it again!

A. M. R. Miller, Chairman, Centenary Committee, EDGC

Roy Greenaway, Centenary Captain.

Message from the Centenary Captains

In this our Centenary Year it is important that we pay a tribute to those who had the foresight to embark on the formation of the East Devon Golf Club. Many people have played their part over the last 100 years in the development of the course and clubhouse and without their forward thinking, sound judgement and dedication we would not be enjoying the benefits and amenities of such a beautiful course and its traditional clubhouse.

A great deal of hard work has gone into the preparation of the Centenary Programme by the Centenary Committee, under the expert chairmanship of Michael Miller, and we owe them a great debt.

We must also pay a great tribute to Kathleen Harland and to all those people who have contributed by helping to record the history of East Devon Golf Club in such a fine book. It has taken almost three years of concentrated effort and they are to be congratulated on such a tremendous achievement. The book will stand as a permanent memorial to all those who helped to make East Devon Golf Club what it is today.

May we all look forward to our Centenary celebrations – a year to be remembered and enjoyed by everyone.

Jill Miller, Centenary Lady Captain.

CHAPTER 1

The Beginning

THE FORMATION of East Devon Golf Club owed a great deal to the drive and initiative shown by two men, Mr E. F. Chamier (1848–1916), the Land Agent for the estate of the Hon. Mark Rolle, and Captain Robert G. D. Tosswill, a retired army officer. Mr Chamier's role was to obtain the permission of the owner to develop the land at West Down for a golf links and thereafter to maintain liaison between the estate and the club. Captain Tosswill's role was to choose the layout of the holes and to organise the work force on a day-to-day basis.

The Hon. Mark Rolle, second son of Lord Clinton, inherited the Bicton Estate in 1842. With foresight and energy he worked to improve the attractions of both the park and the manor. He was also responsible for the building or restoration of churches at Otterton, Budleigh Salterton and Beer and was involved in most of the developments taking place in Exmouth in the late nineteenth century. His interest in modernising and enhancing the locality meant that he was open to the suggestion of creating a new golf course on his land. Golf was immensely popular and in late Victorian times there was an explosion of interest in the game, leading to the formation of many successful clubs.

Budleigh Salterton was no different in this respect. In November 1893 Mr Chamier alerted the Hon. Mark Rolle to the fact that there was a movement in the town to found a club "to make links on the rough ground between Salterton and the flagstaff, at present mostly heather and furze".

The Honourable Mark Rolle

Edwin Chamier

Forty members had been recruited, each paying a guinea fee. This development, however, alarmed a Colonel Walker, living at Lee Ford, who held the shooting rights over the moor at West Down and was extremely reluctant to give way to golfers. He also felt that a new links, so near to the Exmouth links, was unnecessary and would also "bring a number of idlers into the neighbourhood who would be sure to wander about as seemed good to them". The plan got as far as posts being driven into the ground to mark out the land but was then given up, not only because of the colonel's opposition but also for financial reasons. Chamier wrote to Walker, "The golf links on your moors will, I think, be abandoned for want of funds". And so it proved. The ground at Otterton Old Park, which in any case had always been a possible venue, was less difficult – and therefore less expensive – than West Down to convert to a golf course.

BUDLEIGH SALTERTON GOLF CLUB

The Budleigh Salterton Golf Club, with the same forty subscribers, came into being there the following year, 1894. The site was on the east bank of the River Otter, over the high ground above Clammer Bridge, commanding extensive land and sea views. It had a small but sufficient clubhouse. Its president was the Hon. Mark Rolle and its treasurer Herbert Russell, a local bank manager. By 1895 membership had risen to sixty-two. The course was at some distance from the town and access to it was a circuitous one through the village of Otterton. Mr Chamier resigned from the club in 1898, finding "it impractical to go so far to play". An additional disadvantage was that the course comprised only nine holes. So on both counts there was some dissatisfaction amongst the golfers, which led to the possibility of a move being discussed.

The impetus for action came about through a meeting between Mr Chamier and Captain

Entry for The Golfing Annual 1895 – original Budleigh Salterton Club entry

Club Directory. 173

BUDE.

BUDE AND NORTH CORNWALL GOLF CLUB. INSTITUTED 1891.

Entrance Fee, 2*l*. 2*s*.; Ladies, 1*l*. 10*s*.; *Annual Subscription*, 1*l*. 1*s*.; Ladies, 1*l*. 1*s*.; *Number of Members*, 50. *President*--H. M. Freeling. *Committee*--Major Miles, J. King, Rev. G. Wingate, C. M. Cowie, I. J. Llewellin. *Hon. Secretary*--Rev. E. P. Hebblethwaite, Poundstock Vicarage, Stratton, North Devon Mail.

Green Record, 76, by F. G. Johnson, in August, 1895.

A new course of eighteen holes was laid out by Tom Dunn, the Bournemouth professional, in January, 1895, and he pronounces it a very excellent green in every respect, the leading features being the number of natural hazards, and the excellent quality of the turf. The round extends to about three miles, and fine views are to be had from it. There is a separate nine-hole round for ladies of fully a mile in length. Some of the holes are over 200yds., so there is ample scope for long driving. There is no crossing on either of the courses. A new pavilion has been erected at a cost of 600*l*., and there is a resident professional, W. Jeffery (Westward Ho). The nearest railway station is at Holsworthy (L. & S. W. Railway), eight miles distant, thence by coach to Bude. There is plenty of accommodation to be had close to the green.

BUDLEIGH SALTERTON.

BUDLEIGH SALTERTON GOLF CLUB. INSTITUTED 1891.

Entrance Fee, Ten Shillings and Sixpence; Family ticket for three, 1*l*. 1*s*.; *Annual Subscriptions*, Family ticket for three, 2*l*. 2*s*.; Playing Members, 1*l*. 1*s*.; Non-playing Members, Ten Shillings and Sixpence. *Number of Members in* 1895, 62. *President*—Honourable M. Rolle. *Committee*—Captain A. Cooper, Dr. T. G. Evans, Lieut.-Col. H. J. O. Walker, A. P. Percival, F. V. Leese, Captain R. G. D. Tosswill, Miss Hutchins. *Honorary Secretary and Treasurer*—W. W. Rhoades, East Budleigh, Budleigh Salterton, East Devon. *Greenkeeper*—T. Elliott.

Club Prizes.--Club Monthly Medals (handicap) for ladies and gentlemen, finals in December.

174 *The Golfing Annual.*

Medal Winners in 1895.—Gentlemen: W. W. Rhoades, 52 + 50 = 102 – 12 – 90. Ladies': Miss Fosswill, 54 + 48 = 102 – 30 = 72.

Record Scores in Club Competitions.—Gentlemen: 77, by V. S. Leese, on October 7th, 1895. Ladies (over ladies' course): 85, by Miss Theobald, on February 1st, 1896.

Record for Green, 39, by V. S. Leese, on October 7th, 1895.

The course, of nine holes, is about a mile and a half round, and is situated on the high downs of Otterton Old Park, on the beautiful Bicton Estate, the property of the Honourable Mark Rolle. The turf is old sheep pasture covering a light gravelly soil, hence it is dry in all seasons. The hazards consist of hedges, ditches, and a valley, steep hill slopes, stone walls, and clumps of large trees. The putting greens vary considerably, and are generally good, while the "lies" throughout the course are fair. Much care is bestowed on the course, which is increasing in popularity as it becomes more generally known. The views, both seaward and inland, are simply exquisite. We know of none finer. At Budleigh Salterton, about a mile and a half from the course, good hotel, boarding and lodging house accommodation may be obtained. Exmouth (on the L. & S. W. Railway) about four miles from Budleigh Salterton, is at present the nearest railway station. Omnibuses run to and fro frequently during the day. The new line of railway, which is now being rapidly constructed by the L. & S. W. Railway Company, from Tipton on the Sidmouth branch to Budleigh Salterton, will probably be completed during the year. Green tickets are issued to visitors at ten shillings per month, and three shillings per week.

BULUWAYO (MATABELELAND).

BULUWAYO GOLF CLUB, INSTITUTED JANUARY, 1895.

A nine-hole course has been laid out, and as there is a numerous English community, the Club bids fair to be a great success.

BUNDORAN.

BUNDORAN GOLF CLUB, INSTITUTED AUGUST, 1894.

The course, of nine holes, is situated on the seashore at Bundoran, about three miles from Ballyshannon. In a short time it will take rank as one of the best in Ireland. Nor is golf the only attraction, for the beach at Bundoran is magnificent, and there is excellent salmon fishing to be had in the river Bundrowes, and trout fishing in the famous Lough Melvin, which is about two and three-quarter miles off. Visitors may use the course for three days free, and afterwards on payment of two shillings and sixpence a week. Bundoran is 400yds. from the green, and there is plenty of accommodation for visitors in hotels and lodging-houses, while the Irish Highlands Hotel is in the centre of the green itself.

Tosswill, who wished to keep the Land Agent informed about a tree-planting scheme he had organised during 1898 in front of the houses, then recently built, along Station Road. Both being golfers, the talk must have turned to their favoured sport. The Annual General Meeting of the Budleigh Salterton Golf Club was scheduled for a few weeks ahead, in mid February 1899. Both agreed that, if a move were to be put in hand, then the best way forward was to have the projected site surveyed and reported on and then put a resolution to the members of the existing club, proposing the idea of a new links. They must have been fairly certain that the idea would be approved, which, indeed, was what happened.

East Devon Golf Club

A preliminary survey, or what was called "walking the ground", was made in the same month over the high land to the west of the town, centred on the flagstaff on the cliff top. The intended site was moorland, comprising furze, gorse and heather. Chamier's friend, Mr C. E. Pine-Coffin, a member at Royal North Devon, who was to make several more visits over the next three years, joined Chamier and Tosswill. The task at this time must have entailed plotting a way through the undergrowth to rough out the placement and direction of the fairways and also taking note of the rise and fall of the land and of additional features which could be incorporated into forming suitable golfing challenges.

In the next month, March, the Professional at Woking Golf Club, A. P. Martin, arrived, with the blessing of his committee, to carry out a closer survey. This was because Captain Tosswill believed that the links at Woking were similar in character to the one he was planning. Martin's report, written after several days' inspection, gave food for thought. He considered that Tosswill had underestimated the cost of the work to be done. "To get it for twice the figure quoted would be doing well." He went on:

"I do not say it cannot be done, but think the more money there is spent on the rough ground, the better chance of success. Whatever you do, have done well. There is plenty of top dressing close at hand and also good turf which is far better than seed."

While on holiday in Devon later in the year, Martin visited the site again, when he expressed "unqualified approval" for the work in progress.

In April a report was received from Suttons, the seed merchants, who had been asked to confirm the viability of the plans already made. Naturally their advice was confined to the sowing of the greens, where they recommended plenty of lime, two or three bags to each green. Tosswill planned to buy the seed from Exmouth for about two shillings a bag. He also planned to burn the grubbed out heather on the sites of the proposed greens.

Access to the new course was considered. At this time, May 1899, Smart's Hill (later changed to Sherbrook Hill) was in existence. Tosswill and Chamier discussed the possibility of surveying "a first rate road", giving a gradient of about 1 in 15, that would run from the Exmouth to Budleigh Salterton Road, up the incline to meet Smart's Hill and continue on to the neighbourhood of the flagstaff (part of this plan was realised as Northview Road). Tosswill thought this road could be "very easily and cheaply" made. His enthusiasm echoes down through the years: "It would make the prettiest drive in the neighbourhood!"

Photo: Charles Edward Pine-Coffin

The Railway

At the same time as Captain Tosswill was surveying a possible road, Chamier was talking to officials from the London and South West Railway Company. There had been a branch line from Tipton St John to Salterton since 1897 but the line to Exmouth had at this time not been laid. (It was extended in 1903.) Clearly, a successful golf course required easy access, which would be greatly enhanced if the projected line could be laid to Exmouth, within easy reach of the links. It was realised that the neighbourhood could then be developed for housing near the twin attractions of golf and railway. So the estate pressed for a platform to be built at Knowle Hill for the use of golfers and Chamier even considered: "whether it will not be worthwhile to build the Professional's house not far from that point with a small pavilion made out of the materials of the old Salterton Clubhouse, so that golfers arriving at that point may be able to start playing almost immediately. It is a valuable suggestion and one which cannot by any means be neglected." It would not have been a novelty. Halts built for and used by golfers were to be seen on many main lines – for example, Western Gailes in Ayrshire, and Woking. However, the railway's directors were not prepared to co-operate. (Looking some years ahead, the railway company played a more constructive role, being "very liberal in its terms to golfers" who could buy cheap tickets when going to play from nearly all the stations on the local line.)

The Decision Made

By June 1899 attention had turned to a water supply. The firm of Le Grand and Sutcliffe was contacted to provide information on their drilling and boring apparatus. There were worries, however, about getting the tackle up on to the high ground and no drilling for water took place. Instead, the amount of water held in the Sherbrook Reservoir was checked.

By the middle of the month the experimental work on the land was finished. Labour costs amounted to £44.18s.11d. It had gone sufficiently well for official approval to be given for the completion of the course.

CONSTRUCTION AND DESIGN OF COURSE

Not a great deal is known about how Captain Tosswill chose to place his fairways and greens. Presumably he worked with the lie of the land: where vegetation was sparse, a fairway might evolve; suitable grass might provide a site for a future green. By the amount of carting work involved, it appears that large areas had to be cleared of unwanted gorse, heather and stones. The difficulty of the work can only have been increased by the fact that from the highest to the lowest point was a vertical distance of 200 feet. Large quantities of soil had to be brought to the site. It was always a trouble and expense getting suitable soil for top dressing and Tosswill was always on the look-out for sources. One idea he had was to take soil from cultivated fields adjoining the course, which should have been in a better state of tilth than that on common land; yet, on the one occasion when it was tried, from a field of turnips, the results were unsatisfactory and he had to look elsewhere. In 1902, when Palmers were building a road near the newly built clubhouse, the future Links Road, he asked for the best black soil that was dug up.

From the beginning, he gave at least some of the holes names: "Linhay", "Thorntree", "Sherbrook Valley", "Ponds", "Punchbowl". The first three were on the eastern side of the course, the latter two in the dip to the west of the flagstaff.

The Greens

The greens were given a great deal of attention. Tosswill took to heart Martin's advice: "What I should advise would be to go on burning, springing, top dressing, ready for sowing in September, as Autumn sowing comes stronger than Spring. Sow your greens in October which will give them the winter to recover."

Seed was bought from Suttons and by late September 1899 most of the greens were sown and the seed coming up well. Some potential sites for greens, such as the 13th, required drainage before work proper could begin. Here, about 425

View of West Down from the Coastal Path, c. 1900

pipes were laid, of 4 inch and 2 1/2 inch diameter, before being covered with stones and the final dressing of topsoil prior to sowing. A specialist drainer and his team provided by the Rolle Estate carried out this work because the labourers normally employed did not have drainage tools. Two other greens, the 9th ("Ponds") and the 7th ("Punchbowl") needed similar work.

The 9th Green "Ponds" hole, c.1905

These greens, sited on grass fields leased to farmer Maunder, were low-lying. Over the winter of 1899–1900 the drainage ditches were kept open to check on the effects of heavy rainfall. This revealed the need for more pipe-work at the 13th green, together with the problem of water from a spring near Maunder's Linhay (in the vicinity of the present 9th fairway). In the main, however, the work that had been done in the autumn of 1899 held good.

By spring 1900 it was time to put a light roller on the greens. One was procured from T. Beer of Salterton at £19.9s.6d. This was the two men's normal way of working. Captain Tosswill was daily on the site so it was he who identified requirements, whether in men or materials. These requests were put in writing to Chamier who then organised the delivery, usually from local sources. Two rollers were used initially, a light one for the seeded greens and a heavier one for the heathland. Three horses were needed to pull the latter and even that was not one too many as a fourth had to be used to help them up the hill.

The initial work had gone so well that in early January 1900 Tosswill declared that "a first rate nine-hole course could be perfectly ready for play by the end of the month, should Chamier wish it". This had been achieved in only a year. Tosswill himself was in favour of the course being used, firstly, to recoup some of the expense and secondly, because he felt "golfing will do more good to most of the course than any amount of paid labour". However, the idea was not adopted and work continued for another fifteen months.

Problems with Livestock

One cause of delay was dealing with the local tenant farmers whose land adjoined the new course and whose livestock – cattle, donkeys, sheep and horses – were allowed to roam over newly seeded ground. In this respect, the greens on the far side of the course, beyond and below the flagstaff, were a particular problem. Some thought was given to fencing them round or to installing hurdles to hold the animals, but neither method was foolproof and could only be useful in the short term. The problem – that cattle and golf could not co-exist on the same land – was to continue right through the 1900s. Locking the

The course layout taken from Mates Illustrated, Exmouth, 1902

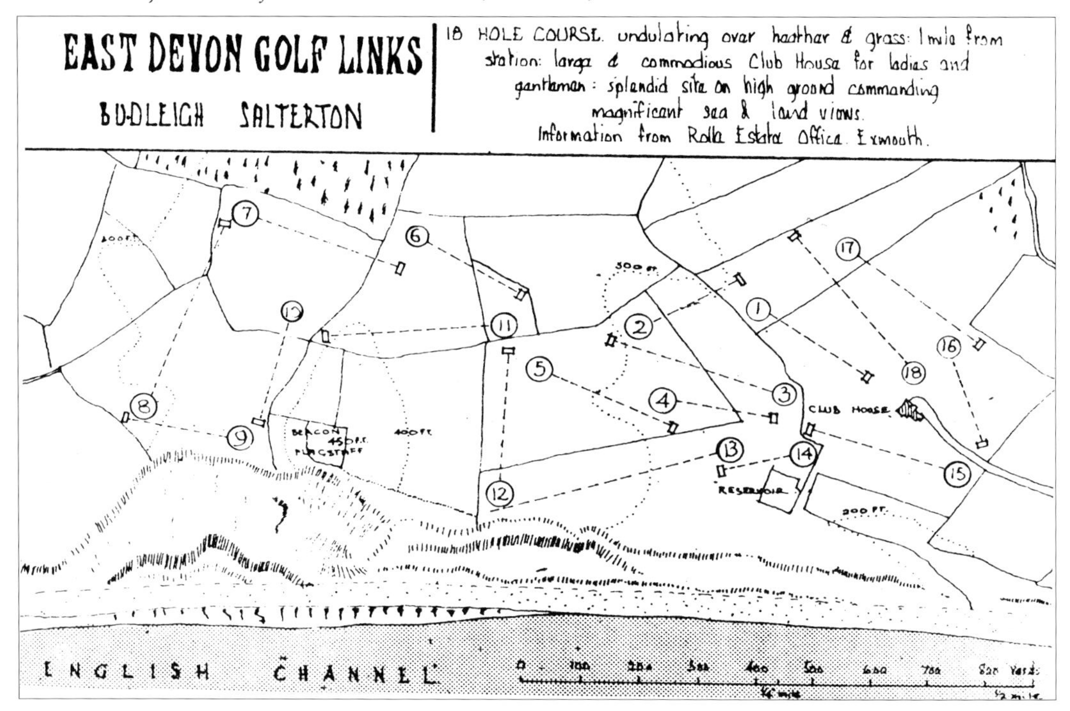

gates from the various tracks that led up on to the moor was tried, and was, in the end, successful, but the farmers proved resistant to changing their habits and gates tended to be left open, deliberately or otherwise.

Another feature of the course's design which caused a problem was the fact that 2 1/2 acres had to be annexed from a nearby farm in order to create the 6th tee and the 11th green. Although agreement was reached with the farmer in early March 1900, his cattle continued to stray. Also the land near the Punchbowl hole became a mass of cart tracks, and promises to keep animals off the newly worked areas were not kept. It took some time for the tenants to adjust. Tosswill told Chamier: "Mr Perriam considers that I ought to rent the moor if I want to use it for golf purposes so he evidently does not clearly understand the position." The problem was partially solved by Tosswill's gang of workmen keeping an eye open for strays and by Tosswill employing a man to look out for cattle on Sundays. In July a kissing gate was ordered to replace the five-bar gate on the edge of the cliff which led from the grazing land on to the course, but this took time to make as all the woodwork on the links was carried out by the Rolle Estate and had to be fitted into the normal work pattern. As the year went on, Captain Tosswill's exasperation grew, until one day he fired off a telegram to the Rolle office at Exmouth: "Horses as usual this morning in Punchbowl Field!"

December came and still animals were prone to wander perilously close to the newly established greens. By this time a man was being paid round the clock to look after the farmer's cattle – and if it was not his cattle, it was his sheep, breaking through gaps in the hedge of the turnip field in search of sweet pasture. Eventually the kissing gate was installed, fences were erected or repaired and the farmers most affected came to accept the course as part of the local landscape.

Foxes and Rabbits

There were, however, other dangers to the fledgling course: the hunt! It transpired that the 7th, 8th, 9th and 10th greens were all under threat from a gallop by the East Devon Foxhounds, whose normal line of run was from the lower plantation of trees up towards the cliff edge. In this case a letter from Mr Chamier to the Master seems to have averted disaster.

Much less amenable was one of West Down's indigenous inhabitants: the rabbit! Scattered throughout the correspondence of the time are irritated references to rabbit depredations.

"The brutes are swarming and delight in spoiling the newly made land."

"Incessant scratching on the newly sown greens will spoil our work altogether. The trapper says that there are no rabbits there. Trappers always say the same!"

"Rabbits unusually active!"

"Do continue the slaughter of rabbits."

With regular shooting, ferreting and tarring of the holes, the problem was contained, but even today the rabbits are on the course – and no doubt they always will be!

Local Employment

The building of the course brought employment for local men, used as casual labourers for digging, carting and sowing. They came not only from Salterton but also from East Budleigh and Littleham.

Numbers varied according to the season and work in hand. Probably about fourteen men was the maximum number working on the course at any one time, though others, such as carters, were employed off-site. An average total weekly winter wage bill was £5, rising to £10 in spring and early summer and peaking at £20 in August.

Necessary supplies also came from the neighbourhood. Lime was brought from Exmouth, firewood from Knowle Hill, gravel from Webber's field or the beach, fertile soil from Short Wood and stone from Tidwell Mount. The timber on the links came from the estate woods. Several five-bar gates, four kissing gates, twelve sets of steps, plus fencing to mark off the cultivated fields were all made from this local wood.

Captain Tosswill, as we have seen, felt that a nine-hole course was ready for play by January

The 4th hole, 1903

1900. More than a year later, in April 1901, he declared the full eighteen holes completed – that is, two years and four months after work had started.

CLUBHOUSE DESIGN AND CONSTRUCTION

Consideration was first given to the building of a clubhouse, or "pavilion" as it was called in the early days, in July 1899. In the autumn David Carr, a London architect, who was engaged in other work for the Rolle Estate, visited the proposed site. He brought with him a preliminary plan. Tosswill noted with horror that things were "not in perfect proportion: for instance, the men's dressing room is smaller than the ladies one"! Apart from general discussions, Carr pointed out the advantage of providing accommodation for a caretaker in the main building instead of in a separate cottage. He promised to send some sketches for criticism. Chamier assured Tosswill that Carr combined "the artist and the architect".

The plans however, did not arrive until the summer of 1900. Chamier suggested that Carr should seek guidance from other golf clubs concerning the size of the rooms, but otherwise nothing else was achieved that year. By January 1901 Chamier, becoming anxious, tried to hurry things along by sending Carr maps showing the levels of the ground and drawing lines to show the angle of view which commanded all the greens in sight from the proposed building. He asked for plans to be sent quickly, writing, "we want to open the end part of May".

Chamier's Concerns

This was not to be, however, since Carr was ill and plans could not be forwarded to the Hon. Mark Rolle until March. There seemed little chance of them being accepted, as they were judged "too expensive and elaborate". Chamier wrote: "Besides, the links will pass into the hands of a club instead of being kept in hand by the Estate."

Meanwhile, Palmers, who were building a nearby road, delivered a quantity of bricks on to the course and Tosswill inquired plaintively as to where he was expected to put them! In July another firm of architects, Boulton and Paul, was asked to put forward plans to be compared with Carr's. As can be seen from the figures below, the dimensions of Carr's rooms were greater.

Rooms	Carr	Boulton & Paul
Luncheon room	28 x 19	20 x 15

Club room	29 x 17	20 x 14
Dressing room	22 x 12	20 x 14
Ladies' room	15 x 18	16 x 12
Kitchen	15 x 13	12 x 10
Pantry	9 x 7	10 x 5

(*All dimensions are in feet.*)

Carr's design also included a "large circular bay". His design was preferred and from that time work proceeded swiftly. By early November 1901 the roof area was finished, "a great relief to Palmer's mind". The building of the pavilion provided much employment for local firms such as Palmers, Sharps and Webbers. A whole range of craftsmen was used, including carpenters, tilers, masons, plumbers, glaziers, gas-fitters and bell-hangers. Chamier praised the quality of the wood in particular, writing: "Palmer has picked out such a beautiful lot of stuff for the joinery (the best I have ever seen) that it seems almost a pity to paint it." Much of it was "best Archangel sawing".

Working Methods

The cartage details give a glimpse of how such work used to be carried on:

Trips to the sawmills
Drawing 79 kerb stones from Knowle Hill
Going to Exeter "after windows"
Carrying a stove from Tidwell Mount
Pulling load of "blue stone" from Cranford Avenue
One horse "clearing up rubbish around the building".

It was the railway (using the line from Tipton St John) and then the horse that brought the materials to the site. The supply of gas was a modern touch. Work for February and March 1902, bringing gas from the company's main pipe to the clubhouse cost £24.

There was some discussion about the colour of the paint. Chamier did not think that Mr Rolle would agree to white paint because of the expense and also the labour of keeping it clean. He proved to be right. Palmer suggested shades of a sage green, similar to that in Chamier's office. But that proved a problem too, because when the glass was put into the roof of the veranda that ran along two sides of the building it darkened the interior and a lighter shade of paint had to be chosen.

Finally, Chamier was forced to put an end to further work. He wrote to Carr in March 1902: "Please don't send me any more details for the clubhouse. We have run out of money and can't execute them. As it is, I shall get into serious trouble, I fear!" The final cost of the clubhouse was £2595.15s.11d.

Clubhouse Amenities

After Opening Day, Carr came down "to see how the place is looking" and he and Chamier lunched at the club. They must surely have felt pleased with their efforts. Freeman's Exmouth Journal called the pavilion "a broad, agreeably

The Clubhouse in 1902

proportioned gabled building in the form of a bungalow and presents a picturesque appearance". There was a terracotta-coloured tiled roof, and a fence of fir poles to mark the boundary. A covered veranda and stretch of lawn invited the taking of al fresco teas.

The interior spoke of money and taste. One of the principal ground floor rooms was a spacious clubroom for the sole use of male members. In future years this room, used today as the Secretary's office, was to become a warm and comfortable den, an "inner sanctum". In winter its inmates – most of retirement age – would sit around a good fire enjoying their drinks brought in on a tray by a white-coated steward. There were newspapers and periodicals to read and stationery was provided.

The other principal room was the lunch and tea room, to which ladies were admitted. Like the clubroom it too had French doors opening on to the veranda. Both rooms had fire surrounds and mantelpieces of fine white Beer stone from the Rolle Estate quarries.

The men's changing room, a drying room that Tosswill had asked for, and a kitchen with larder and scullery completed the downstairs quarters. Upstairs was the ladies' dressing room and two rooms for the use of the club's Professional, L. J. Searle of Exmouth, whose workshop was part of the main building. Care had been taken in the positioning of the clubhouse, which commanded views across nine holes of the course and scenic vistas similar to those elsewhere.

Thought had also been given to the access to the club. The railway station was built in the town and it was arranged that buses would run from there on a newly constructed road up to the links. For those intent on arriving independently, a bicycle shed was provided.

PREPARATIONS FOR OPENING DAY

As work continued on the land and clubhouse, other arrangements were put in hand. Mr Chamier sent out a circular letter of invitation on 18th May 1901 inviting interested persons to a meeting to be held on the course on the 23rd.

The Hon. Mark Rolle did not attend the meeting, which was addressed by a relative, Mr Charles Trefusis, the present Lord Clinton's great-great-grandfather. It transpired that the future members of the club did not wish to lease the ground. Tosswill commented that:

"All looked forward to having good golf at their own price which practically amounted to 'nil' or very little more, while Mr. Rolle should keep up the course in first class order on what money the players chose to contribute."

Mr Trefusis, with tact and courtesy, had put forward Mr Rolle's offer and sought opinions, but did not make any firm commitment. There the matter rested.

At about this time the name 'East Devon Golf Club' was chosen and by the end of the year consideration was being given to the rules of the future club. When Tosswill received a draft copy in 1902 he thought the rules served their purpose admirably as Mr Rolle's rights were made clear but without "any display". He felt, however, that the right of the estate's Land Agent to have a seat on the future committee should have been written in. This is, indeed, what happened. Later on, Lord Clinton had two representatives on the committee.

At this time posters were distributed advertising the imminent opening of the course. Earlier, when cold weather had delayed work, Chamier had told Tosswill: "We must be opened and be clear of the place by the end of March. Mr. Rolle will not have it stand over any longer." The course, to be opened on Easter Monday, 31st March 1902, was advertised as being "3 1/4 miles round with a large and commodious clubhouse".

Terms of Membership

Entrance fee: Gentlemen – one guinea; Ladies – half a guinea.
Annual subscription: Gentlemen – two guineas; Ladies – one guinea & a half, if within 15 mile radius. If beyond that radius: Ladies and Gentlemen – half a guinea, and a further guinea green money.
Application forms for membership were obtainable from Mr Chamier, who was acting as Secretary pro tem. In recognition of his major contribution to the design and construction of

the course, all fees were waived for Captain Tosswill. Sadly he did not live to enjoy these privileges as his health had been failing for some time. He died peacefully on 6th January 1903. Chamier feared that the heavy burden of supervision had weighed considerably on both his body and his mind.

The New Course

However, the fruits of Tosswill's work were there for all to see. In late March 1902, prior to the opening, a journalist from the Devon and Exeter Gazette was invited to walk the course. He enthusiastically praised everything he saw and reminded his readers of the situation of the new course between the town and the prominent West Down Beacon, used as a signal station during the wars against Napoleon in the early nineteenth century. Also at West Down was a coastguard's look-out with nearby flagstaff, so that this part of the Down was known as 'The Flagstaff'. From the vantage point of this ridge magnificent views were afforded in all directions. To the east the coast stretched away from Budleigh's pebble beach, via sandstone and chalk cliffs to the great arm of Portland Bill enclosing a bay of shadowed water. Inland was the rich mosaic of uplands, green pastures and dark woods. To the west was a view of no less beauty. There was the same blue sea, the same clear-cut coast, from Littleham Cove and Exmouth to Teignmouth and Berry Head, and the same richly wooded interior. On the far side of the silver expanse that was the River Exe lay Starcross and Powderham, the graceful slopes of the Haldon Hills and, just discernible on the horizon, Haytor Rocks on Dartmoor.

As far as the course was concerned, there was much to notice and admire. Guided by Mr Chamier in company with a gentleman "whose skill at golf is only equalled by his enthusiasm for the game" (possibly Mr Pine-Coffin or his friend from Westward Ho!, Mr Dunsford), the journalist was directed towards its main features. First, there were the greens, "smooth lawns of yielding turf. Could they ever have been anything but what they seemed?" Their large size was a matter of "general observation", together with the fact that some were termed "sporting greens". The Punchbowl hole was selected for special notice as

Above: The clock in the Pheasant Room.

it had been described by Martin, the Professional at Woking, as being the most interesting of the eighteen holes. Other features that would be noted by the quick eye of "the man with the club" were the exceptionally short distance necessary to walk from green to tee and the fact that there was no crossing on the course "so that the mind of the golfers may be fairly easy on the thought of spoiling the shot of a fellow enthusiast by his receiving the ball against his head!" Another positive factor was the ability to keep the course 'clear' since, being built on private land, it was interrupted by only two rights of way.

As opening day approached, the members of the existing club near the town, the Budleigh Salterton Golf Club, learned through their Secretary, John Oliver, with whom Mr Chamier had been in contact, that they would not be charged an entrance fee should they decide to join the East Devon Golf Club in the course of the year. In return, the 'old' club offered to the 'new' club the pavilion and five shelters in use at Otterton Park, which were accepted with much pleasure. A clock was presented to mark the occasion of the old club 'putting out' and the new club 'driving in'. To this day it still keeps good time in the clubhouse.

The First Captain

The decision as to who should be the first Captain of the new club had already been made. It was to be Mr Charles Edward Pine-Coffin who,

EAST DEVON GOLF CLUB,

BUDLEIGH SALTERTON.

This Course of 18 Holes, $3\frac{1}{4}$ miles round, with a large and commodious Club House, will be opened on Easter Monday, the 31st of March.

TERMS OF MEMBERSHIP:

ENTRANCE FEE—

For Gentlemen elected before 31st March, 1902, One Guinea.
For Ladies elected before 31st March, 1902, Half-a-Guinea.
(After that date the Entrance Fees will be raised.)

ANNUAL SUBSCRIPTION—

(DUE 1ST APRIL)

For Gentlemen resident within a radius of 15 miles of the Club House—Two Guineas.

For Ladies resident within the same radius—One Guinea and a Half.

For Ladies or Gentlemen resident beyond that radius—Half-a-Guinea; and a further Guinea—Green Money.

Members abroad for the whole of any year will not be liable for Subscription for that year.

Forms of Application for Membership can be obtained from the Hon. Sec. (pro tem.),

E. F. CHAMIER,
Rolle Estate Office, Exmouth.

March 4th, 1902.

Original notice of course opening.

as we have seen, had made regular visits while the course was being laid out and who had given Captain Tosswill the benefit of his advice and encouragement. He came from a very large North Devon family. His grandfather, the Rev. Charles Pine-Coffin, originated from Lynton and it was his son, Charles Samuel Pine-Coffin who moved to East Devon and who was the father of Charles Edward, born in 1857. The surname, though possibly appearing unusual, is to be found in many parts of Devon and elsewhere in England to this day. Locally, there are many place names which include Pine or Pyne and Coffin itself is not an uncommon name either. The two names together represent the joining of the two separate family lines some 200 years ago.

Charles Edward read law at Cambridge although he never practised, as his family was self-supporting. He married Olivia Cole and the couple had three daughters, Norma, Olive and Nina. They lived in Exmouth in a house called 'Stoke Lyne', which is now a hospital for handicapped patients. From there the family moved to a dwelling called 'Seacroft', which is now a hotel in Exmouth. Having been an all-round sportsman at Cambridge, Charles continued his prowess into adult life, becoming, as well as a top golfer, one of the best shots in Devon. In addition, he and his wife won many tennis tournaments all over the county. Royal North Devon Golf Club has a very large trophy presented by C. E. Pine-Coffin and, of course, East Devon also has its own Pine-Coffin Cup. Charles Edward died in 1917. It appears that his nearest living relation is his grandson, Dr Anthony Scott-Langley of Upton-upon-Severn, Worcestershire.

Opening Day

On opening day – Monday, 31st March 1902 – a large number of ladies and gentlemen assembled to witness the first drive, which was made by Charles Edward. By that date ninety members had joined the club, though it was expected that the number would soon reach three figures. So, a little more than three years after the conversation between Mr Chamier and Captain Tosswill on the possibility of a new course, they had the satisfaction of seeing it 'teeing off'.

The natural features of the course, which they and others so much admired, are still there for us to enjoy today. Over the years the course has been cared for and developed in a way of which its founders would surely have approved. East Devon Golf Club has maintained continuity with its past.

CHAPTER 2

Development of the Course over 100 Years

AT THIS POINT it will be useful to see how the course has changed over the years as some of these changes are referred to in subsequent chapters dealing with the general history of the club. The opening course layout for 31st March 1902 is shown on the Mates illustrated map. Tosswill's early plans, however, were to start at the hole which became the 17th – in fact where our 1st hole is today! Although we have no card for the course at this time, we can probably deduce from early maps that it was somewhat as follows:

Hole	Yards	Hole	Yards
1	315	10	175
2	100	11	230
3	230	12	160
4	160	13	430
5	250	14	130
6	160	15	260
7	300	16	185
8	360	17	200
9	150	18	340
	2025		2110

Total: 4135 yards

This first layout is far removed from that of today but there are features of the original layout which the observant golfer may be able to detect. Most noticeable is the two-tier green of the 4th (on the present 12th fairway) and the tee of the 6th (on the present 9th fairway). Evidence of the 6th green (in front of the present 8th tee), the 11th green (on the present 9th fairway) and the 7th tee (in the heather – three-quarters of the way up the present 8th hole on the left) is also apparent. This 7th hole was known as the Punchbowl and was regarded as the most interesting by A. P. Martin because it was from a raised tee, with extensive views over the Exe, and played as a dogleg round a pond. The 6th hole was described as having lovely views to the east, red cliffs changing to white, and as the hole crossed the ridge at the top of the course, having extensive views over the Exe.

The longest hole was the 13th, which ran where the 17th is now, except that its green was in the dip at the bottom of the hill (*see Colour Section page 65*). The 14th was a short hole played

Gentlemen putting on the 15th green, c.1903 (on the present 18th fairway).

The 4th green 1902. It had become the 13th green by 1908.

to the reservoir green (its tee presumably the flat area of ground near the bottom of the present 17th on the right, now full of gorse, where many a sliced second shot is nowadays lost).

The 15th had its green just beyond the clubhouse on the present 18th fairway, and the 16th, a short hole across what is now the car park, was played to the practice green of today.

During the first six or seven years many changes, both large and small, appear to have been made, although their exact nature and timing is somewhat unknown. The following references have been found.

1. January 1903 – a bunker and new green built at the 10th.
2. January 1904 – course to be lengthened by some 1200 yards during that winter (Golf Illustrated).
3. January 1906 – discussion about new greens and course by the Punchbowl; levelling Punchbowl green and field (this area must have always suffered from wetness, which was only finally overcome when play in this area was discontinued in December 1914).
4. October 1907 – two new holes are to be played in the newly laid out field (probably the field containing the present 4th green, 5th fairway and the bottom of the present 9th).
   Course Bogey 78.
   Out 4, 4, 5, 4, 5, 6, 5, 4, 4 = 41
   In 3, 6, 5, 3, 4, 4, 5, 3, 4 = 37
5. October 1908 – the alterations advised by Braid and Taylor to be carried out. (Details unknown).
6. March 1909
   Course Bogey 78.
   Out 4, 4, 5, 4, 5, 6, 5, 4, 4 = 41
   In 3, 5, 5, 4, 4, 4, 5, 3, 4 = 37

In a Daily Mail article written in 1912, Colin Aylmer, a local player and the course record holder, went on to say regarding golf at Budleigh:

"The facilities for golf at Budleigh Salterton are by no means as good as they might be. There are far too few trains, and the connections from both the Exeter and Sidmouth sides are shockingly bad. However, once on the course all tiresome things vanish, for from every point of the compass magnificent scenery meets the eye.

"The course is some 5,500 yards long with a great variety of play in it. The first four holes and the last six always seem to me the most interesting; they have a nice 'downy' turf while the remainder are a clay subsoil, very hard in summer and very wet in winter.

"There are some really excellent holes notably the 3rd, 13th, 16th and 17th, and the last two, coming at the crucial point in the round for a close match, make a really capital finish. The 3rd, 340 yards long, requires a very well placed tee shot and a good iron shot on to a very tricky double terraced green, which takes a lot of finding, to register a par 4 [the present 2nd hole]. The

The 6th, c.1925

13th is a very pretty one shot hole with the cleek or spoon 190 yards across a valley, a really testing shot with terrible whins for a bad slice; in fact, trouble is everywhere. To my mind it is by far the best hole on the course [the original 1902 4th hole, whose green is now on the 12th fairway].

"The 16th, 460 yards downhill all the way is the long hitter's delight, for two really good ones will get him home, but they must be deadly straight, as the fairway is narrow, with the heather and furze on either side [the present 17th, but with the green in the dip]. As to the 17th, a mashie or any sort of iron shot will encompass this distance of 140 yards, but the shot must be held up a good ten yards to the left of the pin, as the green has a very big slope running down from left to right [the original 14th reservoir hole].

"During the coming winter the 6th, 7th, 8th and 9th holes will be closed. They are all on clay soil, and it is next to impossible to bring them into a fit state of play [presumably the four holes on the lower west side of the original course]. So it has been decided to make two new holes and these are under construction. The first of these will be played from beside the tenth green in the direction of the flagstaff, a drive and a pitch of 275 yards in length. The second will be an iron shot 150 yards on to the present ninth green. [This was probably the birth of a hole which has developed into our present 8th.]

"I have written about the merits of a few holes, but what about the others? Some are moderate, others mediocre, and one or two are really bad holes. Take the 9th for instance; and there are others of a similar nature. A high bank guards the green making the approach absolutely blind, at least so far as the intervening ground up to the hole is concerned, for I will admit you can just catch a glimpse of the top of the pin. This class of hole is so limiting, whereas be it opened up, the player has the choice of a 'run-up' shot or the 'pitch' if he prefers, and all the time he is seeing that very important thing – the bottom of the pin. The progress of golf stops for no man and the 'management' must continually spend money on golf construction work – every year and for years to come."

It would therefore appear that in 1912 the 1st hole was the short hole across the present car park, with the tee near Golf Cottage, the Professional's shop at that time. The 2nd, 3rd and 4th were our present 1st, 2nd and 3rd, though of a lesser length. The finish was as the original design envisaged by Tosswill, with the short reservoir 14th having become the 17th and the 18th finishing green being overlooked from the clubhouse veranda.

Mr Alymer's plea for improvements seems to have been taken to heart as, early in 1913, the Secretary, Mr R. C. N. Palairet, in conjunction with Herbert Fowler from Westward Ho! acting as consultant, drew up plans for improvements to the course. This involved designing new holes which have provided the basis of the course layout today, i.e. the 6th, 7th and 15th.

In August 1913 it was reported that the 'Hearts Delight', 'Cottage Garden' and 'Flagstaff' fairways had been cleared and were ready for Suttons to start work. The new holes were opened officially on 4th December 1914. After these changes the first seven holes and the last four appear to have remained much as they are now. The 8th hole was shorter and the present 10th therefore did not exist. Players went straight from the 9th green to what is now the ladies' 11th tee. The hole across the valley was the 10th, and the short hole was the 11th to the flat areas on the present 12th fairway. The 12th tee was up on the ridge on the left, now covered by gorse and trees, the hole being played to a green near the present 12th green.

After the First World War the famous course designer Harry S. Colt completed the basic design and layout of the course, which is the one largely played today. He acted as consultant during the whole of the 1920s. His services cost fifteen guineas per visit. The use of Mr Colt as adviser eventually produced a clash with the committee in February 1925 over whether conditions warranted the closure of the links. Major Gay believed that "the management of the course is under the Rolle Estate who will be advised by Mr H. Colt and their instructions will be carried out by the secretary. Colt to visit from time to time." In reply, Mr Foster, Lord Clinton's Land Agent wrote:

"I am sorry that the committee still feel aggrieved re the closing of the course although I suppose there are hardly any courses in England which have been closed for such short periods owing to the abnormal rain, and no doubt a good deal of damage has been done to this one by playing when the ground was sodden. From previous experience a Green Committee has proved not only unsatisfactory but very expensive and Lord Clinton has definitely decided that the management of the course shall be under Mr Colt whose supervision from time to time, although it entails a fee, is cheaper and in every way better for the course than the management of an amateur committee with even the best of intentions. The detailed control of the course, which includes opening or closing, must be left in your hands with the approval of Lord Clinton's representatives and any matters of importance are under Mr Colt's direct instructions."

This plain speaking, which would have been passed on to the members, seems to have settled the issue at least for the time being.

THE 1920s ONWARDS

Early in the 1920s, before 1925, the 8th green was taken further to the right by H. S. Colt and deep cavernous bunkers built on its lower side to catch any ball that fades too quickly down the slope to the right. H. S. Colt laid out the nine-hole ladies' or relief course in the early 1920s. The relief course was sometimes used in winter along with the 18-hole course to form a winter 18 holes. For example, in 1929 the winter course was:

3, L7, L8, L2, L3, L4, 6, 7, 8
15, 16, 14, 9, 10, 11, 12, 13, 17

an interesting order, which can be pictured today.

1925 The hollows to the right of the 10th green were sand bunkers. "The scarlet bunkers produced by the red sand was an attractive feature to the visitor from beyond Devon. The sand was obtained from a pit local to the course, it stayed in the bunkers despite the local winds, comfortable to be in, and good to get out of." (Bernard Darwin)

1926 The ladies' course was opened and the L.G.U. fixed the scratch-score at 74, with the bogey and length of the holes given as:

Hole	Bogey	Yards	Hole	Bogey	Yards
1	4	294	6	3	168
2	5	415	7	4	284
3	4	189	8	4	351
4	4	317	9	5	352
5	4	320		37	2690

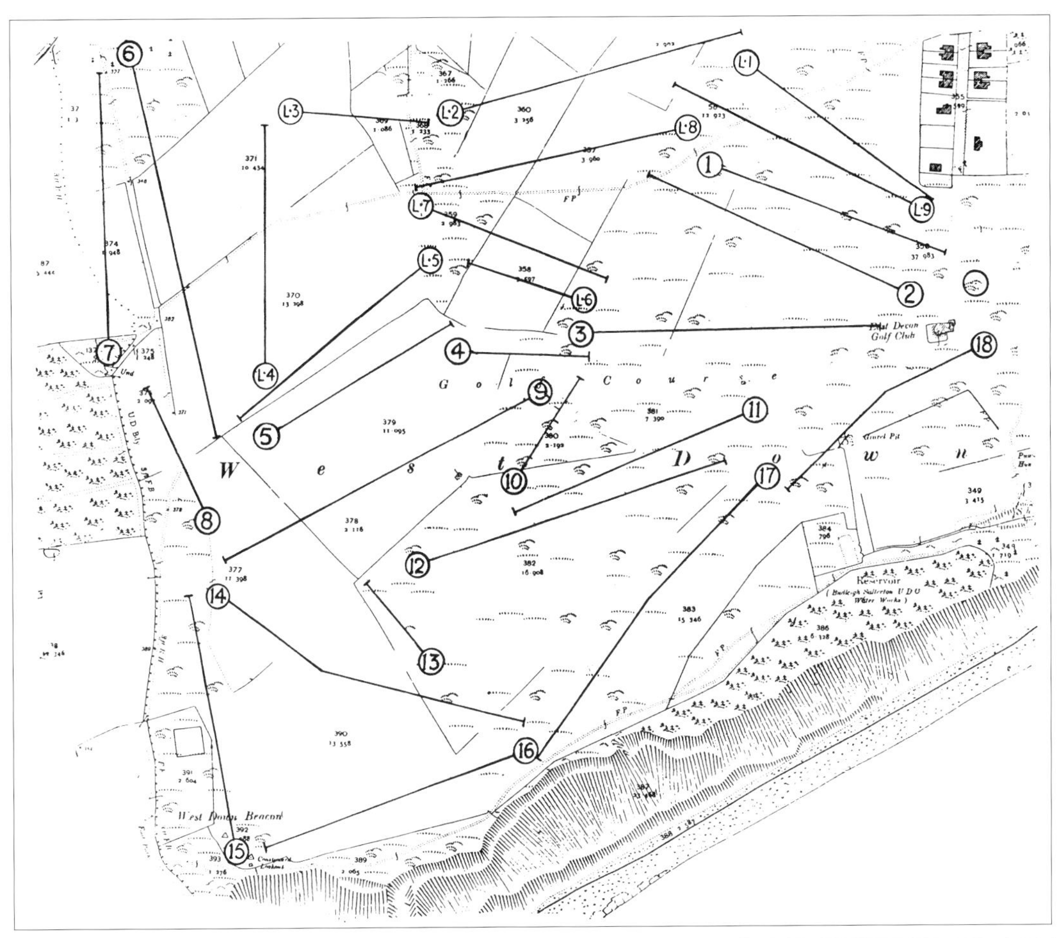

Above: Plan of East Devon Golf Course, c.1926.
Right: The 1920s course card.

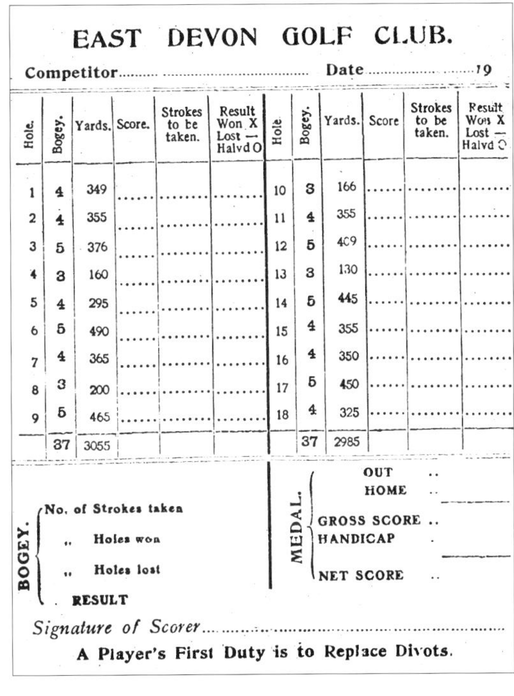

EAST DEVON GOLF CLUB.

Competitor.. Date 19

Hole.	Bogey.	Yards.	Score.	Strokes to be taken.	Result Won X Lost — Halvd O	Hole.	Bogey.	Yards.	Score	Strokes to be taken.	Result Won X Lost — Halvd O
1	4	349				10	3	166			
2	4	355				11	4	355			
3	5	376				12	5	409			
4	3	160				13	3	130			
5	4	295				14	5	445			
6	5	490				15	4	355			
7	4	365				16	4	350			
8	3	200				17	5	450			
9	5	465				18	4	325			
	37	3055					37	2985			

BOGEY.
No. of Strokes taken
" Holes won
" Holes lost
RESULT

MEDAL.
OUT ..
HOME ..
GROSS SCORE ..
HANDICAP .
NET SCORE ..

Signature of Scorer...

A Player's First Duty is to Replace Divots.

1927 The 9th and 17th greens were relaid and reshaped.

1929 The 4th hole was reduced so that the 5th could be extended 40/50 yards. Up to this time the field to the right of the 4th green was out of bounds, i.e. over the bank which exists today. Also in this year, a tractor was first used on the course, replacing the three horses, which had to be hired by the club prior to this date.

1931 A new green and bunkering was designed at the 18th by James Braid. The green to this date had been 20 or so yards further up the fairway nearer to the clubhouse. Sand from the River Otter was used for the top of the 18th green. The red bunker sand came from the Exe and the tee box sand from Exmouth filter beds and the Otter.

The 1st green, c.1925.

The 9 hole relief course seemed to have outlived its usefulness. Major Kitchin wrote to Foster at the Rolle Estate:
"I am convinced that the 9 hole course will continue to be unpopular and as little used as possible until you get rid of its first hole and remove the fierce pull up to the 2nd green. Hardly anyone goes on the relief course now, everybody hoping that everybody but themselves will relieve the congestion by going there, and it is almost a farce

The 5th hole (9-hole course), c.1930.

A. H. WEBBER & SON

HIGH CLASS FAMILY BUTCHER

POULTRY AND GAME SUPPLIED

5, HIGH STREET,

BUDLEIGH SALTERTON.

PHONE 30

Othermo and Wella Permanent Waving. Electric Treatments. Manicure. Marcel and Water Waving a speciality.

DAYLIGHT SALOONS.

CHAS. F. TUCKER

LADIES' & GENTLEMEN'S HAIRDRESSER, TOBACCONIST, ETC.

49, HIGH STREET, BUDLEIGH SALTERTON

Sole Agent for Innoxa Beauty Preparations.

PHONE 203

PARKER'S CAFE

BREAD and CONFECTIONERY, BIRTHDAY and WEDDING CAKES TO ORDER.

MORNING COFFEE — HOT & COLD LUNCHES

AFTERNOON TEAS.

CAKES and FANCIES A SPECIALITY.

49, FORE STREET, BUDLEIGH SALTERTON.

J. & G. ROSS LTD.

LADIES' and GENTLEMEN'S

TAILORS & OUTFITTERS

Shirt Tailors.

227, HIGH STREET, EXETER

TEL.: EXETER 2546

HOOKER & SON

Fish Merchants and Salmon Factors

WHOLESALE & RETAIL.

BUDLEIGH SALTERTON

PHONE 150.

Grams : HOOKER, BUDLEIGH SALTERTON.

Live Lobsters and Crabs a Speciality as supplied to this Club.

HOOPER'S STORES

Groceries and Provisions.

Wine and Spirit Merchants.

Suppliers to the EAST DEVON GOLF CLUB.

13, HIGH STREET,

BUDLEIGH SALTERTON.

PHONE 34

No.	Bogey	Yards	Score	Strokes Recd.	Won X Lost O Halved —
1	4	330	....	**15**	....
2	4	338	....	**9**	....
3	5	407	....	**3**	....
4	3	131	....	**17**	....
5	4	364	....	**5**	....
6	5	491	....	**13**	....
7	4	387	....	**1**	....
8	3	200	....	**7**	....
9	5	466	....	**11**	....
	37	3114			
10	3	150	....	**16**	....
11	4	324	....	**2**	....
12	5	422	....	**8**	....
13	3	126	....	**18**	....
14	5	408	....	**4**	....
15	4	327	....	**10**	....
16	4	363	....	**14**	....
17	5	431	....	**6**	....
18	4	340	....	**12**	....
	37	2891			

OUT ... ... Holes won X...........

IN ... ... Lost —...........

....

Halved O...........

HANDICAP ... Net ....

NET ... ... SCORER

THIS CARD MEASURES SIX INCHES THIS WAY.

Course Card c.1933. The six inch measurement was used to determine a 'stymie', part of the game of golf at that time.

keeping it open, though I suppose it does do a little good. I will await your instructions."

1932 James Braid was course advisor. There was a suggestion to build 9 new holes in the land of the wood to the right of the 8th tee and in the 5 fields to the west of the 15th. This was never done because finances were poor at the time, but had it gone ahead it would have meant a return to some of the land used for the original course layout.

1932 In October the lower men's tee at the 7th was designed, making the hole longer by taking an extra bit of land from outside the course boundary. The original tee still exists behind the ladies' tee and is sometimes used.

1933 A new tee was built for the 3rd. The 3rd fairway was ploughed and reseeded in August.

1934 Braid made proposals for new bunkers on the 3rd which were "met with lots of frigid air when displayed to the committee" and were presumably never implemented.

EAST DEVON GOLF CLUB.
ALTERNATIVE COURSE.

Competitor........................ Date.............. 19'40

Hole	Bogey	Yards.	Score.	Strokes to be taken.	Result Won X Lost — Halvd O.	Hole	Bogey.	Yards.	Score.	Strokes to be taken	Result Won X Lost — Halvd O.
1	**4**	330	......	**13**	....	10	**4**	348	......	**14**	....
2	**4**	338	......	**3**	....	11	**5**	408	......	**10**	....
3	**5**	407	......	**7**	....	12	**4**	466	......	**2**	....
4	**3**	131	......	**17**	....	13	**3**	150	......	**16**	....
5	**4**	319	......	**5**	....	14	**4**	324	......	**8**	....
6	**5**	469	......	**11**	....	15	**5**	422	......	**4**	....
7	**4**	387	......	**1**	....	16	**3**	126	......	**18**	....
8	**3**	200	......	**9**	....	17	**5**	431	......	**6**	....
9	**4**	327	......	**15**	....	18	**4**	340	......	**12**	....
	36	2908					**37**	3015			

PE50383 TOTAL 5923

BOGEY
No. of Strokes taken
" Holes won
" Holes lost
RESULT

MEDAL.
OUT ..
HOME ..
GROSS SCORE ..
HANDICAP ..
NET SCORE

Signature of Scorer..
A Player's First Duty is to Replace Divots.

Alternative playing order, c.1940.

1935 In August all the gorse and heather on the right of the 17th, from the tee to the top of the steep slope, was destroyed by fire.

1937 April: at about this time water was first available to the greens. It was supplied from the upper reservoir with the aid of a water pump. Subsequent quotes from the Secretary show the value perceived:

4.9.37 "The difference in the greens I watered is amazing – no other word is adequate – but alas I am defeated now – no water – it is maddening to think the stuff is watering the sea!"

12.5.38 "Water collected in the reservoir is not enough for drought conditions on the course – double this amount is required for the tees should be watered (they are getting really bad now) and the approaches to the greens would be infinitely better if watered. It is heart breaking to know that lots of water that I sorely need is wetting the sea."

As a result of watering the greens it was thought that the ladies' scratch score might be too high. The ladies 3rd, 5th, 6th, 9th, 12th, 14th and 17th tees were all moved back to maintain a Standard Scratch of 75. This became 74 in June 1938.

1940 In May a new way to play the course was on trial and reported to be a success. Play the

The 9th green and 1st tee of the relief course, c.1930.

present 1st to 8th, then 15th, 16th, 14th, then 9th to 13th, then 17th and 18th. The main argument in favour was the less lengthy period of hill climbing. 5000 new cards cost £5.10s.0d. and the change was adopted.

1943 In July 1943 the War Agricultural Committee had ploughed up the relief course except for the nine greens and two fairways. The expectation was that it would even now, if the war were to end, take four years to get it back into play. This was therefore its final demise. Comments at the time were that: "it never earned its keep though useful at times when visitors were numerous, and for practice, and sometimes in winter for resting 9 holes of the big course. Not popular – too short for long players, too difficult for poor players and has one or two really bad holes, notably the 1st, which gives a bad impression to start with, and the long climb up the 2nd." In September a decision was made not to continue to maintain the relief course except to keep the greens free from weeds. Today most of the relief course has completely disappeared on land which has been ploughed and worked as farmland for over fifty years. However the 1st tee and the 9th green and bunkers can be clearly seen on the practice ground.

THE 1950s ONWARDS

After 1945 very few changes appear to have occurred until 1957 when, under the Secretary, Major Lyle, a new tee was built at the 11th hole. Tees at the 15th, 17th and 18th were also lengthened. The old bottom tee at the 7th, which was designed in the early 1930s, was brought back into use, thus lengthening the hole by about 20 yards. Bunkers in front of the 2nd tee were improved. Apparently the ridge and rough in front of this tee were much higher and tougher than they are today, with a bunker built into the front face of the ridge dating back to 1910 or soon after.

To make early preparation for the likely danger of cliff erosion near the 16th hole, the club invited the well-known golf architect J. S. F Morrison to come down and advise in November 1960. He recommended that the 16th green should be moved some forty yards lower down the slope and more inland on to a patch of ground which had already been roughly cleared. The move would involve alterations to the 14th hole since the 14th Match Tee would then be directly in line with the approach to the new 16th green. This, however, was held to be an advantage as, at the time, the 14th hole was considered the worst on the course. The building of a new tee and the siting of the fairway more to the left (to create a 'dog-leg' and avoid danger at the 13th green) would produce an altogether more interesting challenge. The proposals were costed at about £800. A start was made in the spring of 1961, when earth was bulldozed from the surrounding area of the proposed 16th green to form a plateau on which it would be constructed. The line of the existing fairway was slightly altered to correspond to the new green.

In May 1961 the anticipated event happened. A length of the cliff path near the 16th green collapsed into the sea. As a result the public footpath had to be diverted ten feet inland, parallel to its former route, for a distance of fifty yards. The local council paid for a chain-link and timber-post fence to be erected on the club side of the new footpath.

In the same month the club heard of the proposed diversion of the path running alongside the 15th fairway. The new route – to the east of the reservoir – would bring it to the edge of the area of play. The Secretary voiced his concern that "the whole triangle of the 14th, 15th and 16th will have to be redesigned and the greens moved to new sites". He feared for the amenities of this "notable course" and the subsequent loss in green fees, then running at £2,400 per year.

Specialist advice was again sought. Unfortunately, Mr. Morrison had died since his visit to East Devon and so John Harris of C. K. Cotton & Company was invited down. It was felt that these two men were the "only worthwhile golf architects in Europe". Misfortune struck once more. Harris telephoned to say that his house had been burned to the ground and he was left with only the clothes he stood up in! "We don't seem to have much luck," the Secretary commented.

View from 5th green looking back down the fairway with golfers putting on the 4th green, c.1950

The visit was eventually made and the report received in June 1961. The proposed reconstruction of the 16th hole was approved, as were the existing suggestions for altering the 14th, though for the latter, Harris also recommended extending the green to the right by some ten yards. An imposing bunker would then be built covering the approach to nearly half the widened green, a move which would effectively 'dog-leg' the hole.

As for the 15th, Harris was concerned about recent developments. "It is a disadvantage to have a public path anywhere near a putting green." He recommended that the gorse be encouraged to grow along the right side of the fairway from tee to green and that the green should be moved away from its position near the Beacon. A new large bunker would also be needed in front and the hole in general played well to the left using the existing tees.

Harris's final comment was: "The Budleigh Salterton course is beautifully situated and with some minor alterations could be brought up to modern standards at a reasonable expenditure." The Secretary was more upbeat. The work would "convert three rather dreary holes into exciting golf which could bring the course somewhere near Championship standard, apart from removing the inconvenience of trying to play a serious game before a ribald public". These newly designed holes were largely as they are today and were first opened in the summer of 1966.

In 1971 the top plateau of the 15th green was enlarged "to give us more pin placings and a larger putting area". At the same time a bunker to the right of the 16th green was made larger and a new bunker added on the left of the fairway.

In 1975 the general feeling of the club members was that the 12th hole should be a par five. The golf course architect Fred Hawtree designed a new green and this green was prepared and seeded by July 1976. A further lengthening to increase the SS to 70 was agreed early in 1977, when the 12th was lengthened by 41 yards, the 13th by 16 yards and the 16th and 17th each by 10 yards. This gave the course a total yardage of 6217.

The final major change to date occurred in 1985 when the present 12th was redesigned in conjunction with the advice of Mr Hamilton-Stutt. The bunker on the left of the fairway was introduced and the present green constructed.

CHAPTER 3

The Early Years, 1902–1918

MEMBERS QUICKLY got their feet under the table and the popular drink of the day was soon revealed. "Again the cry is 'no Chartreuse'!" wrote the club's first Secretary, John Oliver to Chamier in May 1902. "There was none yesterday and today I have had a letter asking me to order a bottle in Salterton, but there is none to be had there. Will you kindly send some? Don't you think it would be as well to order a larger quantity as it seems to be so necessary to good golf (!) and there will be a sweep to be played for on Monday next!"

By mid-summer the golfers had moved on to other drinks: brandy, gin, cherry whisky from St Anne's Well Brewery in Exeter, specialist ciders from Whiteways in Whimple, Bass, Pilsner, best Scotch Whisky from Coles, the wine merchant in Exmouth – and yellow Chartreuse! Not surprisingly, the desirability of purchasing a 'Cork Drawing Machine' was soon being investigated. Brisk business meant that a cash register had to be bought and "a book for luncheons and teas" specially printed to help keep track of receipts.

The heart of the clubhouse – at least for male golfers who numbered 170 in 1904 – was the reading or smoking room, which was put to the use for which Carr had designed it: a comfortable den in which to relax.

By January 1904 the clubhouse had a telephone, complete with 'extension bell'. It was not until 1931 that the system was upgraded to provide an extension to the bar for the Steward and another from the bar to the Professional's new shop. The total cost was £12.16s.0d per annum, which, the Secretary was told, "you ought to save out of members' free calls".

1902 Prize meeting announcement for the Club's two oldest trophies, the Pine-Coffin and Rolle Cup..

EAST DEVON GOLF CLUB,

BUDLEIGH SALTERTON.

Prize Meeting, 1902.

TUESDAY, SEPTEMBER 9TH.

The **Challenge Cup**, presented by the President, the HON. MARK ROLLE, will be competed for. Medal play, under handicap. 1st and 2nd Prizes.

WEDNESDAY, SEPTEMBER 10TH., (and following days, as necessary).

Gentlemen's foursomes, under handicap. Entrance 2s.6d. each player, payable at time of entry.

1st and 2nd Prizes. (Entrance fees will be expended for 2nd Prize). Entries close September 9th., at noon, after which the draw will take place.

SATURDAY, SEPTEMBER 13TH.

The **Challenge Cup**, and a Prize presented by the Captain, C. E. PINE-COFFIN, ESQ., will be competed for.

Bogey Competition, under handicap.

Handicaps limited to 18.

JOHN OLIVER, *Hon. Sec.*

Finding Good Stewards

In the early days of the club, finding a good Steward was a recurrent difficulty. The first man lasted three years, the second only one. The problem seems, partially at least, to have been a failure to understand the business of catering, which led to extravagance. Gradually, the proper procedures were worked out. The local tradesmen were informed that no bill against the club would be paid unless a written order from the Secretary was produced for the goods. Succumbing to the temptations of easy access to drink – or 'tippling', as it was called – was another hazard. This weakness may have been the cause of occasional complaints by members and visitors about the attitude and manner of individual Stewards.

Stewards with a drink problem probably did make "too much noise" and offended with their "bad waiting". Members began to think that it would be better for the club to take over the catering and "do the thing properly and reap the profit" instead of relying on independent caterers, but nothing came of it. The Steward's wage in the early years was thirty shillings a week, although it seems there were perks. One Steward kept chickens; another had the profit on mineral waters.

New Ownership

In May 1907 members had the sadness of recording their "deep regret" at the death of their President, the Hon. Mark Rolle. They requested a portrait to hang in the clubhouse. There is, unfortunately, no record that this was ever done. Their expression of sympathy was laid before Lord Clinton and Chamier wrote that Lady Gertrude Rolle would "value the feeling of the members". A set of early Robert Forgan clubs belonging to Mark Rolle were generously donated by his widow and these are now displayed in a glass cabinet in the lounge. The club was promised that things would go on as before for the remainder of the year. In November Lord Clinton, its new owner, expressed his wish that East Devon Golf Club should run "exactly as heretofore". By way of signalling his interest he visited the links and shortly afterwards, in early 1908, the exterior of the clubhouse was painted and several repairs effected.

The Rolle Clubs.

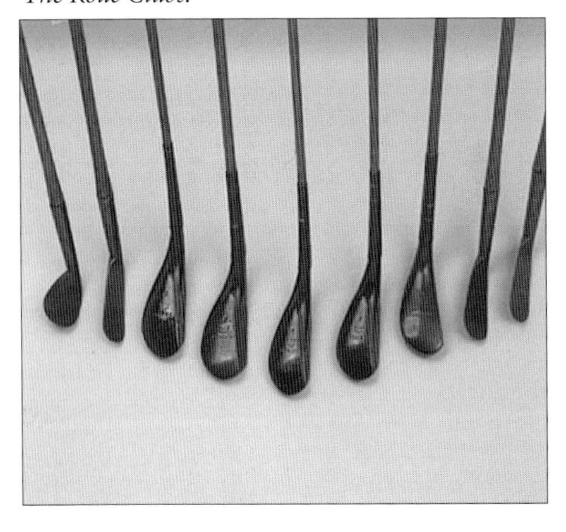

A Clubhouse Extension

In the following year the committee put forward certain "requirements" concerned with the possible extension of the clubhouse, which were on a sufficiently large scale for Lord Clinton to decide "to see the place again". The proposals concerned extending the accommodation for both male and female members.

The enlargement of the men's changing room was achieved by doing away with the Professional's workshop and the caddies' shed. It was planned to "put up a shanty for them off the course". By the addition of the bicycle shed, the lavatories too could be enlarged. The committee, which, in August 1909, had asked for plans of the proposed alteration to be submitted for inspection, recorded in September its appreciation of Lord Clinton's generosity. *(See Colour Section photo on page 67.)*

A Room for the Ladies

Seven years into the life of the club, conditions must have been rather restrictive for its lady members, who, apart from their own dressing room, had use only of the lunch and tea-room. Since male members had exclusive use of the reading room it was decided that in fairness the lady golfers should have their own equivalent. There were, after all, between forty and fifty of them at this time.

What was built was the present day's Pheasant Room, a spacious room overlooking the fairway and the sea beyond. It had a French window opening on to an extension of the existing veranda. David Carr, architect once again, had at first planned for two French windows but as there was "a great deal of complaint" from the gentlemen in the clubroom of draughts from theirs, it was decided that one was ample.

An entrance was made on the east, still the same side by which ladies usually enter the clubhouse. It was through "a nice little enclosed hall", specifically desired by Lord Clinton, who took an active interest in supervising the plans. The hall meant that direct access to the drying room had to be shut off but this was felt not to be a problem since "neither men nor ladies ever go out to the drying room, they only hand their things to the steward or his wife".

In the interests of economy the specification of the internal work had to be modified. For example, "Tudor head doors" were felt to be unnecessary. Wooden casements too could replace "costly iron ones – the last lot alone cost over £80". The internal walls were not to be plastered but left as plain brick. On this point Chamier warned Carr that the ladies "mean to have your blood! (as I told them it was your special scheme.)". In the dressing room a shelf would take the place of dressing tables and mirrors would be fitted over. By October 1909 a contract for £743 had been agreed with Palmers.

In early 1910 work was sufficiently far advanced for the Ladies' Committee to ask to become involved in decorating their new premises. A sub-committee was duly formed, which immediately requested "a small metal or tiled sink or basin" to be fitted in the "new inside room that can be used for washing clubs in". The Ladies' secretary wrote: "It is a great nuisance having them washed in the lavatory basins and we should much like a special convenience for the purpose."

The next month the Ladies' Captain, Miss Morant, wrote to Chamier with a list of proposed furniture. She suggested hopefully, "How about a fender? Can we have tiles?" In the event she received a cheque for £20 for "furnishing ourselves".

Views from the 17th, c.1913, and below a close-up of the distant Golf Cottage and Garage Parking.

In her acknowledgement to Chamier she added teasingly, "I hoped for one fleeting moment when I read yours that you were going to stand us new frocks!" By the end of March 1910 the ladies had possession of their new "inner sanctum". The ladies hoped to take tea in this "new sitting-room" but the idea was turned down by the main committee.

Financial Difficulties

These two extensions to the clubhouse gave rise to consideration of how economies could be effected in its running. The profit for the year April 1908 – April 1909 (when Braid, Taylor, Vardon and Herd played on the course) had been only £40 although, had it not been for the expenses involved in running the Professionals' Tournament, it would have been approaching £220. It was realised that events such as the Professionals' Tournament were excellent advertisement for the club but that, to be consistent and to reap the benefit, money had to be spent on updating facilities, otherwise the links would not be "as valuable an asset to Salterton as they ought to be".

It was difficult not to spend money. The new extensions themselves meant more spending on coal, gas, glasses, crockery and the wages of an additional servant. Four long garden seats were bought to enhance the veranda and a dozen more bentwood chairs from Palmers for taking tea out there. Similar chairs were used in the clubroom.

In May 1910 the water supply began to prove inadequate. Extra help was needed because it required two hours pumping mornings and afternoons to get the water into the pipes. Whytock's suggestion of a windmill to do the job was rejected by the estate on the grounds of being "a horrible disfigurement of the landscape" and being "often inoperable in hot weather when consumption of water is at its height". A 220-watt pump was considered as being "one of the modern ways" of dealing with such a situation. In the end Lord Clinton decided to put in a small oil-powered engine, connected to the existing pumps.

A Progressive Club

Despite the stress of maintaining the course to a proper standard and finding the funds to do it, East Devon was leading the way in the organisation of local golf and inter-club matches. As early as 1907 home and away matches were played against Westward Ho! and in 1910 East Devon beat The Warren team by twelve matches to two. Colin Aylmer made this development known nationally in an article he wrote for the Daily Mail in May 1912.

"Value of Inter-Club Matches."
"In the course of a year there is much golf of interest played at Budleigh Salterton. Besides the summer, winter and spring meetings, there are the usual minor events and inter-club matches, one of which took place last week against The Warren.

"The home side had lost the previous encounter, and in this, the return match, had a very strong side to oppose the visitors. It was rather unfortunate that The Warren were not so well represented as in the previous match, as it would have been interesting to see which is really the stronger club. Probably there is not a great deal to choose between the two, but I am rather inclined to think that our middle men are a shade the better, and would pull us through in the long run. On the day's play Salterton won by 8 1/2 to 3 1/2.

"These club matches are becoming more and more popular. We have such clubs as Tavistock and The Warren going on tour each spring and playing a series of matches, a lead that ought to be followed by many more clubs, as not only do the matches promote an immense amount of interest locally, but the various courses played upon are so different that one has to play "shots" that would never occur on one's native heath."

Although by 1911 total membership had risen to 230, looking back over the dozen or so years since the club's foundation there is a slight feeling that the exuberance of the very early days had subsided.

Like any business, the club would have to pay its way and would have to be regularly modernised in order for it to be able to do so. All too soon a worldwide conflict was to erupt that would make it difficult for these objectives to be realised.

THE FIRST WORLD WAR, 1914 – 1918

When the First World War broke out in 1914, R. C. N. Palairet, Secretary at the time, left for the front and was succeeded by R. W. Friend at an annual salary of £100. The appointment was a temporary one since Lord Clinton valued the help Palairet had given to the club, though he had been in his post only since the beginning of 1913.

In the clubhouse the big question of the day was whether Sunday play should be permitted. A poll taken of the members voted down the idea, not, it seems, on religious grounds but because it would entail extra work for the staff.

However, the war meant that inevitably the military were in greater evidence than before and on several occasions officers came over on a Sunday from their camp at Woodbury, claiming to the Steward that they had Lord Clinton's permission to play. In the summer months this could be dangerous because visitors walked the links in some numbers.

The visitors themselves were another problem. A noticeboard warning that the course was private property had been erected at the Beacon, only to be thrown down with remarks written on it. In 1916 Friend tried to establish from the estate whether there was a right of way across the course. No definite conclusion was reached so the problem continued to occur.

The open expanse of the course was an attraction to the soldiers in other ways. In 1915 the commander of the local Volunteer Training Corps asked permission to use it for trench-digging practice "in some out of the way place", which was allowed. Two years later a 600-yard stretch acted as a firing range though blank cartridges only were used. The only stipulation made was that the volunteers kept off the greens for fear that "they might lie down on them and dig their toes in".

The Coast Patrol – a group of about sixteen men on bicycles who formed a moving look-out – was also accommodated. They were allowed to pitch camp at the back of the 18th green but were warned off using the club's water supply, which was metered.

By way of a further contribution to the war effort the club organised the planting of a field of potatoes which were sold to Bicton Red Cross Hospital. Following the lead of the Tennis Club, wounded soldiers staying in the area, together with a group of Belgians, were offered the use of the course at half the normal fee.

On a less generous note, the Secretary noticed, in early 1916, that several members engaged in war work had not paid their subscriptions though they had not resigned. The idea of remitting their payments was raised but the estate Land Agent, Mr Foster, came down firmly against it.

"Lord Clinton did not start the war and cannot be held liable for the whole expense of it as various people in this neighbourhood seem to think he should be. A great many clubs have raised their subscriptions this year to cover expenses. I have not heard of any instances where subscriptions have been lowered."

At the end of 1916 members learned of the death at Bude of Mr Chamier, who, with Captain Tosswill, had been instrumental in creating the course and clubhouse. Illness had forced him to resign as Land Agent to the Rolle Estate in 1914. His obituary in the Devon and Exeter Gazette bore witness to his "genial disposition" and to the esteem in which he had been held in Exmouth, where he had lived, and in the locality.

Both men would have been pleased to know that their work was being carried on. Although the Secretary reported in mid-1918 that "we are having a very slack time up here" and that "the calling up of men of 41 and over has made a big difference", the profit made in the last full year of the war was £200.6s.0d., which compared quite favourably with pre-war figures:

1906 – 1907: £147.10s.0d.
1907 – 1908: £126.17s.0d.
1908 – 1909: £ 39.18s.0d.
1909 – 1910: £259.16s.0d.
1912 – 1913: £211.18s.7d.
1913 – 1914: £287.4s.7d.

The low returns for 1908 – 1909 was explained by the large fee paid to the Professionals who visited the club that year, as we saw earlier.

CHAPTER 4

The Caddies

CADDIES WERE a feature of golf at East Devon during the first sixty years or so. In 1902 they were given badges to wear to indicate their official status. At that time there were about twenty-four of them. Many were sons of fishermen because, it was said, they got up early. Father would come in from the sea at six or seven and turn out the boys to go and earn some money. Some started as young as ten. Some left at fourteen to get 'proper' work but, if that failed, they would return to caddying.

It was a case of the first caddie to arrive at the course being the first on the course. There was real camaraderie among the boys. Each newcomer to the group went through an initiation ceremony called 'gorsing'. This involved being seized by an arm and a leg, swung high, then flung into a convenient patch of deep gorse – much to the amusement of spectators! During the First World War the Steward, Lewis, acted as Caddie master. He would go outside, blow a whistle to summon the boys and then make out the list of names. His

H.R.H. The Prince of Wales approaching the 9th green, 17th May 1921.

successor was Dicko Brooks who, during the war, had worked at the Voluntary Aid Detachment Hospital in Sherbrook Hill. His dogs were expert ball-finders and always accompanied him. Brooks knew how to turn a situation to his own advantage. On occasion, he would tell a player that no caddie was available, allow him to get halfway up the fairway, then send a caddie after him. When the player returned, Dicko would modestly accept a 'thank-you'!

His job also included collecting the green tickets before visitors went out and he was very careful about it: so careful, in fact, that he kept a spy-glass to hand, which he used to catch anyone starting unofficially on the course. It was he who caddied for the Prince of Wales, the future Edward VIII, when he played the course in 1921.

To begin with, in the 1920s, the cost of a caddie for a round was one shilling if he was a schoolboy or 1s.6d. if he was a regular. One penny out of the money for each round was paid to the Caddie master as commission. This was deducted before the caddies were paid in the evening. Regulars had to be aged fourteen or over and were then guaranteed a weekly wage of 11s. Rounds were counted and when 11s. was reached the money made from the extra rounds was shared out. Around 1920 there were fourteen regular caddies in summer and eleven in winter. By the early fifties the rate had increased to 3s.6d. a round, though sometimes visitors would pay more. No commission had to be paid as the caddie was taken on directly by the golfer. The number of caddies seems to have remained much the same and, as before, they were usually boys in their early teens. If they had not been hired – and in the fifties not many started a round after eleven – the boys went off to the practice ground below the 1st tee to hit a few balls.

For the regular caddies of the twenties and thirties the day began at 8 o'clock, when they were expected to rake the bunkers and, if necessary, bail out any water. Keeping the bunkers in order was a problem because they were filled with red sand which resembled concrete after rain. The sandboxes had to be filled as well so that members could tee up their golf balls on a suitable mound of sand, although the more enterprisng golfers would use slices of hosepipe.

Then it was on to the course, though it was known for some to hide behind the bunkers if caddying had temporarily lost its appeal! The boys were lucky to get two rounds in one day but just in case they would bring some lunch with them – usually bread and jam sandwiches, and cold tea in a lemonade bottle. If a boy was called on to the course these had to be stashed away carefully if their owner wanted to see them again on his return! Mornings gave the best chance of work, though the summer months were busier. Many caddies had their own 'people' whom they usually went out with. Major Gay, Secretary in the twenties, would play three or four times a week and would always take a caddie with him. Usually he played with Arthur Barnes, the Assistant Professional, and sometimes he gave Arthur a caddie. This round was always watched with interest because it followed a pattern. After five holes Arthur was usually two up, but at the turn invariably the positions were reversed and Arthur would be three down. This was supposedly because Major Gay always had a cigarette on the sixth!

WAITING AREAS

When the course was opened for play in 1902, the caddies waited in an 'enclosure' to the south of the 16th tee near the newly built Links Road

Starter's 'Bathing Hut' next to the Caddies side of Golf Cottage and the Professional's shop, 1920s.

Humphrey – the Caddie Master.

(see Mates Illustrated map). In 1909 they were given a new caddie shed alongside the Professional's shop on a plot across the road from the present-day car park. This was known as Golf Cottage at the time of construction in 1905. It was a single-storey building which cost £331 to build. This brought objections from the owner of 'Highfield', the house at the top of Sherbrook Hill. Perhaps he feared noise or nuisance, but the plan went ahead. The hut must have been a cosy enough place to wait in since in winter it was heated by an open fire. In 1930 there was another complaint from 'Highfield' because caddies were gathering behind the Professional's shop and climbing over the fence of the property's boundary. After reference to the lease, however, it was discovered that the boundary was not the fence but the hedge.

It is possible that this incident prompted the club to reposition the Professional's shop. In 1929 there had been a plan for a shop to be built on to the side of the ladies' locker room. In 1931, however, Stickley, the Professional, was provided with a new building on the site of the present one. The caddies were left in their old quarters. By the mid-thirties it was becoming obvious that a new caddie shed was "a din [real] necessity" because they were too far away for proper supervision and tended to "break up everything". So a wooden shed was built behind the Professional's shop, between it and the practice putting green. A tiny office – known in the club as "the new palace" – was created for Humphrey, the Caddie master, and a telephone extension laid on from the clubhouse since it was thought inconvenient for the house staff to have to go outside to see if a caddie was available. Humphrey was then ideally placed to keep the boys "under his thumb". The new quarters, ready by spring 1937, meant that Humphrey's "bathing machine" – possibly a real one or a look-alike which he had used as his personal shelter – could "die a well deserved death".

It is probable that these arrangements lasted for almost twenty years until 1955, when a new trolley shed was added to the existing shed at the back of the Professional's shop. To make way for this, a timber-framed and corrugated-iron lean-to shed was removed. There was a bench inside and it was close to the 1st tee. The caddies' meeting point then seems to have moved to the area now occupied by the Town Club.

STATUS OF CADDIES

One point concerning the caddies that regularly came up for discussion among the club's administrators was personal injury compensation. When the Compensation Act came into force in 1907 requiring the insurance of employees, the club felt it necessary to insure the Steward and his wife, the Professional and five groundsmen but were uncertain about the legal position of the caddies. Golf Illustrated was consulted to see if it had any advice to offer. It seems that Chamier felt that since caddies were surely classed as being in casual employment the Act would not apply to them. It would be different, perhaps, if a golfer employed one caddie regularly during a whole season. There was also the question of whether the Professional was the real employer of the caddies since he received a percentage from each round. Eventually, in 1910, the committee decided to take out a Caddie Insurance Policy at the rate of sixpence a member, which was reviewed from time to time in the following years.

In the 1930s the question of National Insurance became tied up with the question of whether caddies should be 'regulars' or 'casuals'. As we have seen, the club had regular caddies in the 1920s but their numbers seem gradually to have diminished. The practice at other clubs varied. At Weston-super-Mare and Burnham regular caddies were paid wages and insured accordingly. They had to be on duty at a specified time. On the other hand, at Westward Ho! all caddies were casuals and therefore not insurable. They did not have to turn up if it did not suit them. It worked at that club because, as the East Devon Secretary wrote: "Westward Ho! has plenty of poor. We have not." He was in favour of regular caddies because it meant that there would be a dependable supply. As things stood, it was difficult to get enough caddies to meet demand and so Humphrey could never definitely promise one or take a booking for the following day.

By the mid-1930s the regular caddies numbered about fifteen. Their guaranteed wage was 14s.6d. per week, though the average was 16s.7d. This they received whether they 'carried' or not. Health and unemployment deductions were made and fines of 2s.2d. levied for each day of absence without leave. In 1937 the guaranteed wage was raised to 16s. in an attempt to increase green fee and bar takings by making a larger number of caddies available to members and visitors.

In 1943, during the Second World War, casual caddies were used and these did not have to be insured as officially the club did not pay them. Each casual caddie was charged 2d. (if he got a job) for the privilege of trespassing on the course to make money. The player was supposed to pay 2s. a round plus a tip.

Glimpses from the Past

The caddies, of course, were in a good position to study the idiosyncrasies of the various golfers they worked for. There was, for example, the

Golfers with their Caddies at East Devon.

one-eyed man in a striped blazer who hated to lose, particularly on the 18th. Another member, a big-hitter, lost six balls during one round but consistently refused to let his caddie look for them. However, that did not stop him from complaining about his losses and his lazy caddie to the Caddie master at the end of the round.

Another eccentric golfer was one day playing in a four-ball that had reached the 4th tee. He prepared to drive – there was complete silence. He addressed the ball but then cocked his head as if listening to something. "Tick-tick, tick-tick" – "Can't stand that!" he exclaimed. Reaching into his pocket he took out his gold Hunter watch and threw it into the gorse surrounding the tee. It took two caddies all morning to find it.

Another story of 'lost' then 'found' concerns Walter Pursey, the club Professional from 1912 to 1922. Much to the disgust of some in the club, he had become engaged to one of the lady members. Whilst he was giving her a lesson in the practice area, now the 18th green, her engagement ring went missing. He immediately offered a pound reward and all the caddies turned out to look for it. Arthur Robins was the lucky finder. He bore off his sovereign home to his mother, whose first reaction was that he had 'pinched it' but, when reassured, put it to good use by buying a new suit of clothes for him.

Caddies' memories bring back the 'old days' when civilians from India and the Far East, who had retired to the area, played round the course and swapped stories of famine and drought encountered while administering the Empire. There were soldiers who had explored Afghanistan, Tibet and the Gobi Desert. One keen player is remembered as having a fixed twelve-day rota of partners. On the list were nine generals on successive days, followed by two admirals and on the twelfth day – only a colonel!

Not surprisingly, etiquette on the course was rigid. If a ball was lost the group behind simply shouted "Fore!" and played through without hesitation. It was considered a 'crime' to hold anyone up. The greens were treated tenderly. Nothing could be put down on them. The caddies were expected to rest the clubs or the bag on their boots. And how speedy the golf could be! Early starters would be round in two hours. Times change. Nowadays on the course the hum of electric trolleys has drowned out the old enquiry, "Caddie, Sir?".

1920s view of 3rd tee and Clubhouse. The Professional's workshop has not been built. The starter's 'bathing hut' is clearly visible.

CHAPTER 5

Between the Wars, 1918–1939

WHEN PALAIRET returned as Secretary at the end of the war he recorded the following expenses:

Wage bill "on the green": £30.2s.8d. monthly

Wage bill "in the clubhouse": £10.10s.0d. monthly

Hire of horse and man: £8.3s.6d. monthly.

He did not remain long at the club, leaving in October 1920 to be succeeded by Major Gay, chosen by the committee and approved by Lord Clinton. Friend, who had held the fort from 1914 to 1918, was appointed a life member of the club on Lord Clinton's instructions.

SPACE AT A PREMIUM

In the summer of 1927 there was reported to the Land Agent "a movement afoot among the members and committee" with the aim of altering the dining room. Specifically they wanted the dining room moved to the reading/smoking room because the former was over-used. The Secretary, Major Kitchin, set out the problem: "At present people are having drinks at the same time as early lunches have started. Tables laid for lunch are covered with ash, matches, etc. and often have to be re-laid."

The Clubhouse c.1925

He might have added that visitors wishing to pay green fees had also to seek out the Steward in the dining room. This might have been the reason why lunches were not going well. A full lunch cost 3s.6d., lunch with cheese 2s.8d. Even though these were the lowest prices possible, Kitchin wrote "whatever you charged, the local people would not feed here".

It was difficult, perhaps, to plan changes when there was constant maintenance work to be financed. At about this time requests were being made for a new carpet for the smoking room, guttering for the roof of the machine shed to prevent the machines standing in water, the repair of a bad leak in the men's dressing room, the staining and polishing of the parquet floors and the replacement of tiles "lingering above the glass of the veranda". Yet it was beginning to show that space was at a premium. Again, in 1927, the club was forced to find "a proper place to keep the bar stock" which, at the time, was stacked up in the passage leading to the ladies' part of the building. This dump was raided and a certain amount taken following the presence in the clubhouse of "a fairly rough crowd".

Kitchin had plenty of ideas as to how the existing space could be better used, and even obtained estimates, but Foster, the estate's Land Agent, decided to make the situation plain. "I do not think you are likely to get any constructive alterations in the building in view of the fact that you (that is, the club)

Close-up 1920s view of Clubhouse and 'bathing hut'.

already owe the Estate £18,000." It was a very understandable position for the estate to adopt, though that did not prevent Kitchen complaining:

"Catering is down. There is no comfort or reclusiveness in the dining room in August because, during lunch, the late starters come in and drink and the early afternoon players pay green fees. There is an incessant opening of doors and draughts. If you lunched here during August you would enlarge the clubhouse, I have no doubt."

The 1920s, era of the Depression, were difficult times and the golf club was indeed struggling to be profitable. In February 1929 the Secretary apologised for being overdrawn at the bank and having to use an emergency deposit account, "but the last two months have been terrible", he complained. He suggested raising winter green fees to 2s.6d. and summer green fees to 3s.6d. Fees had not been raised since 1921 so his idea was accepted.

THE PICTURE MATCH

The Picture Match, the annual two-leg fixture between East Devon and Sidmouth, dates back to 1932, when the Captain of East Devon, H. W. Adie, received a challenge from "sixteen stalwart fellows" of Sidmouth Golf Club. Adie replied by acknowledging the arrival of these "rabbits", as he called them, and promising that they would be "slaughtered"!

At about the same time two cartoons depicting the event were drawn by a Sidmouth member. These were later framed together to produce "The Picture". One shows an eager team of Sidmouth rabbits making its way over Peak Hill, led by the Sidmouth Secretary, F. H. Carroll. The second picture is drawn at the same spot but this time the rabbits are lying forlornly on the ground, shot dead, and Mr Carroll is walking back alone to Sidmouth. At the present time the score stands at 41 to 22 in East Devon's favour, with several matches halved.

THE THIRTIES

1931 was a worrying year. By December the Secretary knew that the account would be overdrawn before 1st April 1932, yet it was difficult to make a profit when costs were rising. The price of beer was up: Guinness stout rose from 4s.6d. to 5s.3d. per dozen bottles. Should bar prices be raised proportionately? "Our prices are not low now even at the old cost." Always there was the fear

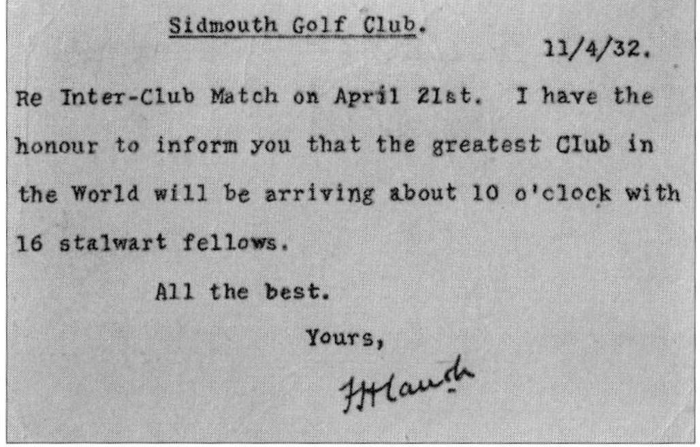

Sidmouth Golf Club.

11/4/32.

Re Inter-Club Match on April 21st. I have the honour to inform you that the greatest Club in the World will be arriving about 10 o'clock with 16 stalwart fellows.

All the best.

Yours,

JHlauch

The Picture.

Shortwood House.
Budleigh Salterton.
Devon.

April 13th/32.

Re: Sidmouth Rabbits. v. Budleigh Salterton [illegible]

I have the honour to receive your epistle of the 11th inst: & note that you are sending sixteen, 16, XVI, (sixteen) Rabbits, which will be slaughtered in due course & returned to you for cremation on Apl: 21st.

Cheerio, all the best.

[illegible]

that takings would fall if prices were increased.

From a financial viewpoint the 1930s were little better than the 1920s had been and in recognition of this some members tried to help. In 1932 a board was presented, on which were inscribed the names of all the Captains of the club since its foundation. It was hung in the smoking room. A glass display cabinet for trophies was donated by another member and greatly appreciated because, up to that point, the cups "had dwelt almost entirely in the Bank".

There was, naturally, a steady stream of repairs: to the chimney stack of the ladies' room where the crows had been nesting; to the rotten timber supports on the veranda; to the lockers of the men's changing room, where many locks had been broken through being forced by a screwdriver, there being no master key; to the dining room walls, "dreadfully chipped"; and to the wooden floor blocks which had worked loose.

Over and above repairs was the need to keep pace with modern developments. The estate put electricity into the clubhouse in 1934. It was made clear that this was an estate matter as the Agent wrote: "Please note that this does not concern the committee." A "cold box" was approved at the same time. This "Frigidaire machine", as it was called, was then something of a wonder. An annual fee of three guineas was paid for "periodical inspections and oilings and breakdowns" but it was considered "a great boon" to the catering.

Two years later, in 1936, the electricity supply was extended to the lighting, which until that time had been powered by gas. It was put in on "the hired wiring system" by the Electric Light Company.

This led to an attempt to boost profits through the catering. Enquiries made at the Rosemullion and Rolle Hotels had revealed complaints from the visitors that no refreshments were available in the clubhouse after a round of golf on Sundays, when, traditionally, only the changing rooms were open. East Devon was considered to be "behind the times compared with neighbouring clubs" who were, therefore, gaining an advantage. The Licensing Laws of 1933 allowed a bar to open for eight hours, beginning not earlier than 11 a.m. and ending not later than 10 p.m. with a break of at least two hours after midday.

It was decided to apply for an extension to open on Sundays. When this began in 1935 it was just for two hours from noon for cold lunches and drinks. The existing staff of Steward and Stewardess, two waiters and two female general servants would take on the additional service.

The following year, 1936, saw the dining room kept open all day on Sundays, as on weekdays, though the sale of drinks did not begin until noon. Since visitors paid their green fees to the Steward in the dining room it was felt that keeping the lunch menu "under their eye" might promote sales. These visitors were to be the main source of business.

The Secretary wrote: "Your local population would not stay to lunch anymore than they do nowadays, which is NIL." Most members were retired. In the 1930s the Secretary identified a youngish man as "one of our few members who work". Among these few was the striking figure of the Reverend T. G. Shelmerdine, vicar of Littleham, and Captain in 1938. When in the reading room he was in the habit of sitting "on what looked liked a throne" but which might possibly have been an armchair! It was he who scored a telling final point in an argument comparing the glories of his parish with those of Budleigh by commenting that even the signposts bore the legend "B. Salterton"!

Since its members were unwilling to support the catering, it is surprising that the club did not take up an initiative proposed by the management of the Rolle Hotel which was trying to attract golfing visitors, who currently made up less than 10 per cent of its clientele.

They put up the idea of giving the club £50 per year in return for which the hotel would receive a roll of green fee tickets with the right to issue them at not more than six every day.

Since the annual subscription at the time was five guineas, this meant that the club would receive £50 for a theoretical six members' subscriptions amounting to £31.10s.0d. Although this seems a reasonable proposition, it does not appear to have been acted upon.

The total Sunday takings for the year ending November 1936 were: Catering – £19.14s.6d.; Bar – £32.7s.11d. Not for the first time, Mr Cole, the financial agent of the estate, had to transfer money into the club's account so that it could meet its bills. "I suppose everyone is busy making money and has not time to spend it," he wrote to the Secretary, rather wistfully.

However, the true reason for the difficult financial situation may have lain elsewhere. The members wished the club to be an exclusive one. Their attitude was surely reflected in a letter written by the Secretary to the Land Agent in 1932.

"Mr _____ has put up for membership here one Mr _____, the new manger of the Rolle Hotel. He brought him up here and introduced him to me and he seemed a very decent fellow. But do we want him? The Rolle Hotel looks to me a 'pub', not a Rosemullion type of hotel and if he is elected why not also the O.C. [military slang for 'Officer Commanding', meaning 'the manager') Feathers and the chemists and butchers and candlestick makers. The man in question I have nothing against. He seemed a very decent sort of his own particular brand. It is really where it may lead us that I am worrying about."

This, after all, was 1932, an era of class distinction and class-consciousness. The club, as it was, suited its members very well and they did not wish to admit anyone who might strike a jarring note. To them the golf club was not a moneymaking enterprise as it was to Lord Clinton's Land Agent.

It is unlikely that they worried about the deficit showing in the bank statement, though the Secretary certainly did. They wished simply to play golf and socialise with like-minded people. Their attitude is further revealed in a subsequent letter written in 1933 by the same Secretary:

"Is it sound for me to get non-Committee people to propose and second the three people for Committee? Might it not encourage members to suggest names of people who would not suit? My own view is that, as members take so little interest, it is wiser to try and let Committee do the job, and as we have a Committee whose views are so entirely 'for the Club's good' I think it is sound to keep the election of Committee members in the hands of Committee. I don't like the idea of Tom, Dick and Harry proposing and seconding people who would perhaps not be good for the club. They are always entitled to do it under the Rules – need we go out of our way to ask them to do so?"

So not only was the club kept within a certain social circle, but also within that circle control was exercised by only a few members who had the desire and the interest to do so. Their main concern was golfing matters; financial affairs were in the hands of the club's owner.

CHAPTER 6

Maintenance of the Course, 1902–1939

IT IS INTERESTING to read how, in the past, the various parts of the course were cared for. Those were the days before modern fertilisers and machinery, so inevitably, techniques were different.

The course had been laid out on a mixture of moorland and pasture and therefore the quality of the land varied. Early on, in 1909, the field going to the 5th hole and returning to the 11th gave cause for concern because of the poor growth of grass. The Secretary, W. Whytock, considered three remedies. The first was the idea of folding with sheep. This had the disadvantage of necessitating closure of the holes concerned while hurdles were brought out for the sheep, which would have to be fed with cake, and hay carted on to the ground. The second possibility was to cover the affected area with farmyard manure but again this entailed closure. As a third alternative, he felt that the ground, once rolled and cut, could be dressed with basic slag at a ratio of 4 cwt per acre. In spring, a further dressing of special grass manure – of which bones were a major constituent – could be added. About five acres required treatment and Whytock estimated that the two dressings would cost about £8.10s.0d. He had wanted to ask for a dressing before but felt he had to keep costs down. He was also "rather sick" of the whole thing "after the unreasonable way in which members complain of the course".

He received a sympathetic response from Chamier whose advice obviously drew on his knowledge of estate management. Chamier felt that folding with sheep, combined with heavy feeding and young seeds trodden in, was the only system that would make a permanent improvement in both plant and soil. Slag, he felt, stimulated what grass there was but did nothing to improve the soil. He even drew the diagram illustrated to explain his method of "layering" – that is, shifting the sheep down the fairway.

Chamier's 'Layering' diagram

Hole 5		
	4	8
	3	7
	2	6
	1	5

Initially Chamier felt that putting this on the course would not be a problem: "the course is so wide – there is plenty of width left for even the worst duffer like myself". However, second thoughts prompted him to come down on the side of trying slag first and no more is heard of the "folding with sheep" method for fertilising the fairways. Clearly it would have caused too much disruption.

IMPROVING GRASS

Constant vigilance had always to be paid, as it still is, to the quality of the grass. Before the First World War "renovating seeds" were ordered by the bushel for raking into bare patches. Road scrapings were mixed in with the seeds. A mixture called "complete grass manure" was also ordered by the cwt. Moss could be a problem. Its growth was put down to wet weather and lack of sun. To combat it lime was used and in the 1920s sulphate of iron was laid down by the ton to encourage the grass to grow. A dressing of sulphate of ammonia, at £1.4s.0d. a cwt. was then applied. Sometimes the damage was extensive. In 1929 the Secretary, Major Kitchin, reported that "the tees have been quite hacked to pieces and many fairways will have to have very considerable quantities of dentists' stoppings rammed in". In response, the estate sent up fifty loads of topsoil and about 150 loads of silt from the River Otter, which, however, required sifting and turning to remove the weeds.

The longish coarse grass, still to be found on the 17th, was more widespread in the 1920s and 30s, covering the 11th, the upper part of the 12th, as well as the 15th, 16th, 17th and most of the 18th. Its growth was self-limiting and therefore it was ideal in the days of a small ground staff relying on scythes and horse-drawn mowers. Additionally, it stood up to drought and frost. It was, however, impossible to take deep divots.

Bringing in Sand

Two types of sand were used on the course. "Fresh" or "lawn" sand was laid as a top dressing on the greens and fairways. It was always supplied by the agent and in 1910 cost 36s. for two cwt. By the mid-1920s annual demand was running at sixty tons. About the same amount was required for the second type of sand, used in the bunkers and tee boxes. When possible this was brought over – a hundred loads at a time – from the Exmouth filter beds. When this source failed supplies were obtained from the Otter. Other opportunities were not missed.

In Exmouth one day, in 1932, while passing the gas works, Kitchin spotted at the base of a cutting a layer of sand two feet high and promptly commandeered it for the course. On another occasion, in 1937, having no sand at all, he went up to the Blackhill Quarry and cast his eye over the l/8th of an inch dust chippings to be had there. He thought they would do the job as they would not "set" or blow away too much, though he admitted that "explosive shots" did, in time, reduce the quantity of whatever was in the bunker. The cost was £17.10s.0d. per hundred tons.

Major Kitchin wrote: "The bunkers at present are an insult to the course. Two hundred tons of sand would do for the bunkers near greens. The others don't matter so much."

"Kitch the Sec."

Upkeep of the Greens

As would be expected, much time and attention were devoted to the upkeep of the greens. Before 1914 the number of green staff varied between four and six, but Major Kitchin also played an active role. He used fish manure on the greens and "orchard soil". He thought it good soil but "not free of seeds of coarse grasses – which will mean tearing our baby sown grasses to bits at some considerable cost in labour". Instead, he preferred to rely on grit for the greens but, once again, not the grit supplied by the estate. His preference was for Teignmouth grit that could be had for £5.12s.0d. per eight tons. This had more body in it than some. Kitchin planned to have it mixed with some soil he had set aside, "safe from coarse grasses" and then to have it laid two inches deep over the top of the orchard soil. He was also willing to use "garden cultivated soil" on the basis that the weeds it might contain were less damaging than the coarse grass seed.

Many of the greens had been built on a layer of rotting gorse and settled into shallow hollows about 6–18 feet in diameter. A high-pitch shot to the green falling on the slope of one of these hollows might break right or left or shoot forwards. Those who could keep their approach shots low had a big advantage.

The 17th green had an additional hazard – the slope up to it, which was full of rabbit holes. A ball which failed to reach the green and rolled back was quite likely to disappear down one of these holes, but keen-eyed caddies were rarely at a loss.

Grit and Dressings

In his quest for quality grit Kitchen extended his search to Ladram Bay. There was not grit worth having in the bay itself, nor in the next bay towards Sidmouth, but in the bay to the west there was some of "excellent texture". However, on speaking to a local fisherman by the name of Staddon, whose father had worked on the course while it was being laid out, he heard that supplies of the grit would be unreliable as it was "there one day and gone the next", depending on the strength of the wind and tide. He was concerned, too, about its salt content though he believed that "salt is a stimulant if used in small quantities". Exmouth river grit was found to be even saltier, whereas at Teignmouth, which he also visited, he could not taste salt at all.

The preference for Teignmouth grit persisted into the 1930s, although Dartmouth grit was also tried. The Secretary took samples from both Teignmouth and Dartmouth to Shand, the local chemist, to test their respective salt content. Teignmouth proved to be the least salty of all the local grits but on one occasion, when the lorry arrived to deliver a load in 1937, it crashed through a drain outside the front door of the clubhouse. However, there was general appreciation that at least a full 10-ton load had been delivered!

Other dressings were also tried. Pearlwort was something new, as was applying peat as a top dressing for "waterless" greens. A few loads from Woodbury Common were requested. It was not an instant cure-all as the peat had to stand for a long time before it could be broken up into powder. Sulphate of iron continued to be a favoured remedy. There is no doubt the greens were as well cared for in the 1930s as they had been earlier.

In 1936–37, for the first time, the practice was begun of dressing the approaches to the greens over an area of 20–25 yards. This had been tried on the 15th hole, which had been "practically dead", with encouraging results. The cost was estimated at £18. When asking for the money, Kitchin wrote: "I think if the approaches had thick coatings of grass the golfing quality of the course would increase enormously in dry weather as the ball would not bounce so much."

Irrigating the Course

In 1936 the question of providing water for the course was being considered and by the spring of 1937 a system was in place. With the aid of a pump water was drawn from the upper reservoir, which the Council had built in 1913 near the flagstaff, and led to various points on the course. This major advance was greeted with "a very hearty vote of thanks" to Lord Clinton at the AGM The following year the pumping machinery was upgraded to give about 15,000 gallons per 24 hours. Kitchin, the Secretary, reckoned he could keep the greens "good" for about ten days in a "complete drought".

But all improvements had to be made against the background of a shaky financial position. Writing in August 1937, which should have been a busy month, Kitchin remarked: "Green fees are not worth a penny stamp for a postcard so far."

Fairway Bunkers

The treatment of the fairway bunkers shows that lavish spending was frequently not an option. Although money had been spent on architects' plans for the placing of the bunkers, in 1935 Kitchin floated the idea of sowing about half of them. The reason was the maintenance required. "They are ludicrously large and take hours of work to weed and scratch." It was a fine line between spending too much, thereby worsening the financial deficit, and spending too little, thus allowing the course to deteriorate.

MECHANISATION

Mechanisation came gradually to the course. Initially horse power was used to pull the mowers that cut the fairways. Specially made leather 'shoes' were used to enclose the hooves to stop the sharp edge of the hoof cutting into the turf and leaving imprints. The club had a pony but it was not strong enough to do the required work once these shoes were put on. It was not always plain sailing since the horses were hired and the men who accompanied them knew nothing about a golf course. "The 'horsy' man knows nothing about green-keeping!" sniffed Whytock, the Secretary, in 1910. At this time the rates for horse hire were 7s. for 7 1/2 hours. Permission for this service had always to be obtained from the Land Agent. Mowers came from the Ideal

Company and from Shanks. In the cost-conscious manner in which the course was run, used-mowers were advertised for sale.

In the late 1920s a band of uncut grass and wild flowers was left at the base of the gorse. Even the light rough was long enough at times to hide a ball and the rich, self-seeding growth encouraged an equally rich variety of birds. For several successive years a skylark nested in the long rough in front of the 10th tee. In a match, should an opponent miss his tee shot it was legitimate gamesmanship to discourage him from looking for his ball. A hawk could often be seen hovering over the cliff.

The First Tractor

In May 1929 the Secretary, Major Kitchin, began a campaign to obtain a tractor for the links. He had been at Exeter Golf Club: "The way their tractor trots about the course made me groan when I thought about our slugs of horses." He presented the acquisition of a tractor as an economy since he felt that the horses were made to walk slowly so that he had to hire three and even then only got an old man and a lazy boy. Besides, it would save on the cost of maintaining the cart tracks. "I know of no course which does not swear by them," he declared.

He did not have long to wait. By August the newly bought tractor was "doing well" and he had begun to worry about where to house it. The shed near the 11th green would take it but it had no doors and, if used, a new home for the carts would have to be found. There was the question too of whether the mower wheels would stand up to the tractor's speed. New, strong wheels would be needed at a cost of 24s. each. The alternative – a vehicle called the Rapid Motor Mower, which Kitchin suggested – was rejected on the grounds of expense. In January 1930 a lorry was approved for the course. In return, Kitchin was asked to try to do without horse hire. Rough gorse cutting, for example, was to be done by scythe.

Mowers

The mower, now tractor-drawn, worked well until 1932 when the Secretary began negotiations for a replacement. He had a good case since it was about twelve years old and was considered, by Carter's blacksmith who inspected it, to be not worth repairing. Two years later a Ransome Triplex was purchased for £90. At the same time a hand-mower was bought from the same firm: it had ten blades but only a 14-inch cut. It was felt that narrow mowers could cope better with the "many small sinkages" on the greens, where wider mowers tended to leave long grass because they did not fit into the hollows. This machine cost £13. A mower with three units was considered but rejected as not providing "those pretty looking lines, alternate light and dark" on the greens' surfaces. To complete updating the machinery, a tractor was ordered from Carter's for £217 in 1936 and another from Bolton's the following year.

WORKFORCE WAGES

It is difficult to discover the wages of the men employed on the course, though there was a correlation between their wages and those for agricultural labourers. A glimpse of the position is given in 1926. Seven men working on the course had written to the estate asking for a rise. Their wages were 30s. per week. Hours were 7 a.m. to 5 p.m. for five days and 7 a.m. to 12 midday on Saturday, with one and a half hours off for breakfast and dinner. This worked out at a 47-hour week. The men were also paid on Bank Holidays and on wet days when work was impossible. The agricultural wage at the time was 32s.6d. a week. The Land Agent, Mr Foster, ruled that since the work done on the course was usually only "boys' work", the existing wage compared favourably and could not be increased.

In 1932 men were still working a 47-hour week on the course and still for 30s. They did not work on Sundays, Bank Holidays or Christmas Day. Winter hours were shorter because of the lack of daylight. The estate's Agent, however, believed the hours insufficient if the link was to be retained with agricultural hours. Farm labourers worked 52 hours a week from April to October and 50 hours a week from October to April – all for the sum of 32s.6d. The club was asked to increase the hours accordingly. The club was also told that the ground staff should work on Bank Holidays and especially the Saturdays before Bank Holidays so that the greens could be in proper order during the holiday periods "when the Green Fee harvest" was expected. The club increased the men's hours to 50 1/2 per week.

Bank Holidays posed a trickier problem since the men were aggrieved at their anticipated loss. The Secretary did what he could. The men were told that they could be called upon to work up to 3 p.m., but that if they worked "extra hard" beforehand, no doubt they could leave earlier. Major Kitchin was considerate of his workforce and was even prepared to accept "flexi hours" years before the phrase was invented. At times of "stress on the course" he thought an early start at 5 a.m. was beneficial so that mowing could be done without interruption. This allowed the men to leave in the afternoon to go to other employment, which some wished to do.

LOCAL DIFFICULTIES

It is not surprising that the problem of animals straying on to the course, met with during construction, should have continued into the first thirty or so years of the course's life. Cattle on the fairways occurred mainly at the low holes. It was a question of maintaining running repairs on the fencing. If this was neglected they broke through and then there was a debate about who was responsible for putting it right. The "hunting and shooting men" were held to blame for gaps appearing. Whytock, the Secretary in 1911, wrote in exasperation: "Hunting so near the cliffs is just a farce!"

At this time the 6th green was particularly vulnerable to animals being driven along the road leading to the five-bar gate. It was also vulnerable to predatory goats kept by a nearby householder, who was apt to tether them too far away from her own garden and too near to the green! Badgers too showed a fondness for this area, coming through the woods from their sett somewhere near the 7th green.

Rabbits continued to take their toll. The trappers brought on to the course never lived up to expectations. One arrived with ten traps to cover the whole area and only stayed a day. Perhaps he knew the futility of the exercise! Another became "distressed" when most of the rabbits caught in his snare were eaten by foxes; whether this was due to his humanitarian feelings or to losing his 'perks' is unknown. At any rate he wanted the hunt to be called in "to draw the cliffs"! Major Gay, Secretary in the mid-1920s, had the idea of paying a man to "clear them once off and then wire the cliffs". This demanding scheme was never heard of again.

Sheep were an occasional nuisance. In 1905 complaints were made that "for some time past sheep have been sleeping, mostly on the 13th green, and have spoilt it a good deal, their urine in this dry weather burning out the grass in great patches. The sheep are also in the habit of sleeping on the 12th green and on Monday mornings it takes two men quite half a day to clean and clear up these greens." The solution was for the farmer in question to fold his sheep at night either on his own land or on other parts of the course, but as in the past, getting the co-operation of the individual concerned was not always easy.

Farmers, who had their own routines, were, as we have seen, reluctant to change the grazing patterns of their cattle or be more punctilious about fence repairs simply because a club, established for sport, had been developed amongst them. Shortly after the First World War a nearby cornfield became something of a battleground. Golfers were prone to enter the field in search of wayward balls. A local rule forbade this practice but it was generally ignored. In June 1920 the farmer was paid £20 in compensation for damage to his crop and notices were placed in the main clubhouse and in the ladies' room about the problem. It may not have been entirely unrelated that in the following autumn the same farmer's cows were found to be wandering on the course, spoiling new seeding, while he himself was "carting daily" across the 8th though there was apparently no need for him to use this route.

As the years passed there were fewer incidents of this kind partly because the course became an accepted feature of the landscape and partly because, after 1914, play on the lower holes, where problems had occurred most frequently, was discontinued. Although one of these holes, the Punchbowl, had been held to be the most interesting on the course, the area where it was sited quickly became waterlogged and proved resistant to drainage schemes. In consequence, the holes were closed for long periods over the winter, which led to over-use of the remaining holes and discontent among the members.

TRESPASSERS

There were – and still are – two public rights of way across the golf links. Littleham Church Path enters just beyond Links Road and goes up to the road between the 6th and 7th holes. There is also the stretch along the left of the 8th fairway, which curves behind its bunker to join the path running along the right of the 15th fairway. This was the stated position in 1931 but it was not so easy to defend in practice. The views from the course attracted walkers and those in search of free firewood favoured the woods.

The stile near the lower reservoir, off the 17th hole, gave admittance to quite a number of people, with and without dogs, and was replaced by a fence. Other walkers took the chance of a short cut across the practice ground. Stickley, the Professional, reported that people were "apt to be truculent when asked to clear off". Worst of all was the area around the 6th green, where cars would be parked and their occupants then proceed to take a stroll along the fairway. It was muttered darkly that if nothing were done "charabancs" would start turning up!

The issue was at its height in the mid 1930s. To repel the invaders three sets of noticeboards were set up at strategic points. These were:

- at the top of Northview Road to direct picnickers away from the 18th green by means of a "PRIVATE" warning;
- at the entrance to the cart track running between the 6th and 7th holes, where a sign pointed "TO THE CLIFF PATH";
- at the 8th tee, where a similar notice was placed.

CONGESTION

The course was not congested in the early days presumably because of limited numbers of members and visitors. However, the general hazards and rough of those days were more ferocious than they are now. One member recalls that "the second tee was separated from the fairway by some vegetation that would not have disgraced Borneo and by a bank like Beecher's with some sand in front of it where now there is scarcely a noticeable undulation". By way of compensation the same golfer remembers "the thousands of butterflies which inhabited the course and how, when you struggled through the heather, dozens of brown and blue ones were put up by every step".

By 1930 a scheme was on trial for three starting places on the course. It appears that a round beginning on the 1st tee of the main course had to start before 9.45 a.m. For those who started after 10 a.m. the round began on the relief course and was completed on the first nine holes of the 18-hole course. Two rounds on the relief course could begin at any time.

Colt's 8th hole was proving to be "a log-jam". It was reported: "It does hang the players up badly and makes avoidable congestion." So more gorse was cut back on the right of the fairway to widen the approach to the green.

Slow play was another possible reason for congestion on the course, but before 1945, at least, this does not appear to have been a problem. A letter on the subject, written by the Secretary, Major Kitchin, in 1938, is of interest:

"On the average I do not think ladies are slower than men in going round the course. I emphasise 'on the average'. There is a sort of competitive spirit arising here that I do not like. It is only amongst a few and they are definitely friends of mine, not people I do not care for. They pride themselves on going round the course in 1 hour 40 minutes and if they play behind a slower couple they come in full of anger. The average speed of the course is about 2 1/4 hours, slower on crowded days, faster on empty days and I think it would be good for 1 hour 40 minute people to learn that 2 1/4 hours is about reasonable. If restrictions on ladies' starting times are abolished, it may cause congestion on the 1st tee, probably resulting in more use being made of the Relief Course."

The question of slow play is still very much an issue today.

CHAPTER 7

The Second World War, 1939–1945

THE FIRST SIGN of the effects of the impending hostilities was noticeable in the summer of 1938 with an increased army presence in the neighbourhood. Sharpshooters' camps were established at Dalditch and the club gave concessions to the officers' messes there. A subscription of two guineas a week covered any number of officers wishing to play. Usually there were about six or eight. The following year the subscription was changed to 10s. per head for the officers of the 68th Field Regiment, who were down for a fortnight's camp. For a keen golfer it was certainly value for money, but the Land Agent remarked, "I don't suppose they will be playing much as probably they will have to do a little more work than usual."

In 1940 the club offered free golf to any member of the overseas armed forces home on leave and a day's play for 2s. for home-based servicemen or women. After the retreat from Dunkirk in June 1940 some officers of the British Expeditionary Force were living locally, on leave. The Secretary classed them as servicemen "who have not been overseas" and liable therefore to pay 2s. This was because "for a time at least it looks likely that they will not be based in France". He was right.

The onset of war caused a drop in membership even in a club where most members were retired. By early 1940 thirty-one full members had resigned (twelve men and nineteen ladies), of whom about twenty-five had been called up. It was agreed that such members could rejoin "at their previous rate of annual subscription" when the war was over. In such a way did the club perpetuate its very varied scale of annual subscriptions. In addition, eleven men and five ladies changed their membership from playing to non-playing. This practice the Secretary encouraged. "Every guinea helps and perhaps we may get a sixpence out of each on bar profits." Membership was also falling at other local clubs, such as the Warren.

ARRIVAL OF MILITARY

The effects of the war appeared on the course itself in the summer of 1940. First to arrive were the Local Defence Volunteers, recently renamed the Home Guard. Their post was at the old 15th green. They arrived for duty in their own cars, which, to the Secretary's fury, left tracks not only across several fairways but even over the new 5th green. In desperation, he sought to protect the green with a cordon of broken bottles. The course at this time had its own "main road" from the clubhouse to the 5th green, but in the dark the drivers either found it difficult to follow or did not even try. Fortunately the Home Guard did not remain for long, its post at the Beacon being taken over by the army. The volunteers withdrew to a position at the bottom of the practice field and the Secretary, who regarded them as "obstructive", breathed a sigh of relief.

The second group to make an impact on the course was the army in the shape of Captain Kelly and his company, who, during the same summer, dug gun pits, made a sandbag shelter at the Beacon, just off the old 15th green, and laid barbed wire along the side of the 18th hole. They also took action against the possibility of enemy aircraft using the course as a landing ground. This was done by erecting stout posts about 3 feet 8 inches high above the ground at intervals of 5 to 6 yards. Four strands of strong barbed wire were then interwoven at the top and stretched between the posts. The aim was to arrest the landing wheels and so tip an aeroplane "base over apex" on to its propellers.

The third and final "assault" on the course by the military happened without warning in June 1941. Two officers, "not of our local troops", arrived at the clubhouse. The major wore a kilt, the subaltern was a Royal Engineer. They informed the Secretary that construction work – of great solidity – was planned at the Beacon. It would be a very "hush-hush" affair. The surmise was that it was something to do with a radio station. When work started the army used the existing track from Castle Lane up to the 8th tee. This was then extended along the left side of the 8th fairway, rounded the back of the 8th green and continued along the right of the present 15th fairway until the Beacon was reached. Inevitably the old track became very worn and the new one – still in existence – became a feature of the landscape. The old 15th green and the old 16th tees were wired in, as was the upper reservoir. When, later on, a leak developed in an uptake pipe, the Secretary had to apply for a pass from 555 Coast Regiment, Royal Artillery, in order to have checks carried out near the reservoir.

The military occupation at the Beacon ended in September 1944 with a notification from the War Department Land Office. The committee agreed that the former 15th hole should be brought back into play. Members also wished to keep one of the Nissen huts the army had erected as a compost and fertiliser store, plus a small corrugated-iron hut for use as a shelter near the 10th green and 11th and 17th tees. The anti-aeroplane posts on the course that interfered with play were then removed, stacked up and the cost charged to the government by way of sending the account to Major Palmer, officer-in-charge of the Budleigh Salterton Home Guard. Other poles and wires, which did not cause an obstruction, were left for the Sappers to remove in due course.

The process of returning to normal continued into 1945. In March the War Department made checks that all the mines were cleared before the land that had been taken over was formally de-requisitioned. At this time there was still barbed wire on the cliff path. In October Lord Clinton approved the committee's decision to cease temporary membership along with green fees for the Services. Land clearance work was still being carried out at the Beacon in May 1946.

THE CLUBHOUSE

In January 1939 the clubhouse was visited by a member of the local council, the object being to see if it could provide accommodation for refugee children from the cities. It was immediately pointed out that the living quarters were already fully occupied. No more was heard until early 1941 when the three main rooms downstairs were inspected for possible use as a school. A letter was composed by the Secretary and the Land Agent, stressing that such a scheme was out of the question. The club had between 300 and 400 members and anything from over 3000 visitors a year. If the rooms were lost membership might dwindle and visitors go elsewhere and since the town provided "practically no other amenity than golf" the hotels and shops would suffer. It was also pointed out that it was government policy to provide "premises such as these for exercise and relief". And finally, quite apart from all this, the lavatory accommodation was totally unsuitable. This broadside silenced all further enquiries.

Major Kitchin maintained an equally robust attitude towards those adult refugees who, he said, "fled to Budleigh Salterton as a safe and sound funk hole". He thought it "just pathetic to see what deep intrinsic value some blokes place on their hides!" Of course, the Major was a veteran of the First World War and a holder of the Distinguished Service Order. This must have coloured his attitude. His own recipe for survival was "to buy a good pair of wicket keeping gloves and try and catch the bomb you fear will fall on you". He wrote light-heartedly but he must have been anxious too. When War Weapons Week came round in May 1941 he organised a collection on behalf of the Royal Air Force Benevolent Fund. He wrote, rather poignantly: "I do want this club, so full of generals, to produce a respectable amount. My boy has now done 30 raids."

Great care was taken to follow the regulations regarding blackout. Police and "specials" were apparently "red hot" in the area and care had to be taken if fines were to be avoided. The changing rooms, the front hall with its skylight, the dining room and staff quarters all received attention. In the men's reading room and the ladies' room the light bulbs were removed and the doors locked. For the duration of the war the only public room that remained in use was the dining room.

Catering Problems ...

The provision of food and drink for members needed thought and planning. As early as the spring of 1940 Kitchin wrote to Mr Cole, who handled the estate's finance, "You had better come along soon before rationing gets worse or your lunch will be – what?". Nevertheless, for a time, the members did pretty well. On weekdays a hot meal was provided with "never less than two veg., often three". There was also a choice of about three cold meats followed by two or three sweets and "the usual BBC [biscuits, butter, cheese]". On Sundays only cold cuts were available but the rest of the menu was unchanged. The cost was 3s., later raised to 3s.6d. All this was achieved with an allowance of 4s.2d. per week for meat plus offal if it could be had. It was a good service, too good to last.

In May 1941 the local Food Controller barred the Budleigh Salterton Tennis Club from serving teas because it did not serve lunches. Since the golf club did serve lunches it was unaffected. But there was a fear that the "self-refugees" seeking an alternative venue might swamp it. A rule was rushed through committee to the effect that no card playing was allowed in the clubhouse and that tea would be served only to playing members and to others playing golf. In this way unwanted visitors were kept out.

This state of affairs lasted until the end of the summer, when the government forbade the serving of meals by any establishment which could not prove the provision of twenty meals a day, which the club could not do. The Secretary noted disconsolately that he would have to try to sell off tins of food to the members, but then cheered himself up by posting a notice in the tradition of the British spirit in adversity: "No meals served after Saturday next. No objection to nosebags!"

...But not with Alcohol

On a happier note the supply of alcohol was maintained throughout the war. The club made its own ginger beer, costing about 1s. per dozen bottles and selling for 4s. per dozen. But by far the most popular drinks were whisky, gin (Plymouth and Booths) and sherry. Sales were practically at pre-war levels. A 25 per cent profit was made but even then the drinks sold below pub prices. Thought was given to building up stocks – French vermouth, for example, was difficult to obtain – but "the very faint risk of one chance bomb" put an end to the idea. Strangely, there does not seem to have been any alcohol rationing until after the war. In July 1946 the committee ruled that members should be limited to two drinks per day – two small whiskies, for example, or two medium tankards (not pints) of beer. It was solemnly decided that the drinks need not be the same. It would be allowable to have a Guinness followed by a sherry – though why anyone should want such a combination was not explained! It was, thankfully, a temporary measure.

There was something of the air of "make do and mend" in the clubhouse throughout the war. The premises became damp but coal was scarce. Four thousand bricks of black Irish peat, well dried, were bought instead for £19.5s.0d. In 1944 a new stove was acquired for the dining room. This proved "excellent", excellent being defined as "very economical": one large scuttle of boiler nuts kept it going, day and night, for forty-eight hours. Gradually the clubhouse became less used. From spring 1943 it was closed at 6 o'clock instead of at 8, not only to help Stickley, acting as Steward, Professional and Caddie master, but because there were simply not many people about.

WARTIME SHORTAGES

Two factors affected the proper maintenance of the course during the war years: lack of staff and lack of fuel.

Staffing Problems

Just as some members were called to the war, so were the ground staff. At the end of 1940 only one man remained to work alongside Mears, the greenkeeper, and Dale, the tractor driver. The rest

F Stickley (Professional)

were "children". In 1941 Stickley took over Caddie master duties while remaining Professional. For this he was paid an extra £78 per annum, which, with his £100 as Professional and £150 as Steward, brought his salary above the £300 paid to the Secretary. Kitchin resented it but in wartime adaptation was a necessity. Later in 1941 Mears was called up, leaving Dale and five "lads" to care for the course. Letters were written to the labour exchange at Exeter, representing that neither Dale nor Stickley was "A1". However, in late 1942 Dale was ordered to go to Palmers to drive a lorry and Kitchin was left with "7 lads under 18" and badly wanting "a man to control them". Dale returned in 1943 and used the occasion to have his salary increased to £3 a week and no insurance to pay. The boys' salaries ranged from 30s. to 48s.2d. a week, being tied, as in former years, to the agricultural wage even though they did not work such long hours as a farm labourer.

The winter of 1943–44 was the lowest point for staff numbers. Only one boy remained and the Secretary was reduced to asking the estate if any members of its Exmouth Office could help. "They must be able to push a mowing machine and stand up to rather severe weather." There is no record of this tempting offer being accepted! Overall it has to be assumed that the lack of expert attention over a number of years must have had an adverse effect on the condition of the fairways, greens ands bunkers. On a more positive note, however, play was never suspended during the war.

Shortage of Fuel

A hint of what was to come was given in January 1940 when the government requested details – as it did nationwide – of all petrol-driven machines used on the course. These comprised two tractors, one Dennis lorry and one Atco hand mower. Shortly afterwards the Regional Petroleum Officer, an official whose job it was to assess the fuel needs of local firms and establishments, sent out the first of many sets of coupons which dictated the amount of petrol that the club could use during the following two months. The coupons went first to the estate, which forwarded them to the Secretary, who cashed them in for petrol. For April and May 1940 the club was allowed 100 gallons. Since this represented one third of the previous year's consumption for the same period it is not surprising that the allowance was declared "hopelessly inadequate". Yet the pattern was to be repeated throughout the war and indeed was to worsen, as the figures below reveal:

June and July 1941	72 gallons
June and July 1942	52 1/2 gallons
June and July 1943	36 gallons
June and July 1944	35 gallons

For any two winter months, 20 gallons was the usual allowance. Appeals occasionally produced a little extra but never more than 10 gallons. The estate suggested – probably only half-jokingly – that members might be interested in a Manual Lawn Mower Handicap, once round the course, once a week, but the proposal fell on deaf ears.

It became impossible to maintain the fairways of the relief course, though efforts were made to keep the greens cut. In May 1941 potatoes were sown there for the first time and in the following year more ploughing was undertaken. Once again the greens were made an exception on the grounds of expense. It was estimated that it would cost £400 to re-establish one green. Littleham Church Path was also avoided since it was a public right of way. The difficulty of maintenance eventually brought an end to the relief course.

On the main course there was nothing for it but to return to the old method of propulsion – horse power. A man was found to come in on occasion, bringing two horses and a wide cutter. This "kept down" the areas most necessary for good golf and in return he was allowed to keep the hay. By the middle of the war, however, petrol was so scarce that it was forbidden to use the Atco manual mower. So the appearance of horses on the course became a regular feature and a real necessity. It cost £5 for the cutting of "all that really mattered".

The war years brought difficulties for the club. Development and improvement of the course were impossible. It took enough energy and initiative just to carry out basic work. In the clubhouse the amenities were under-used and this caused a sizeable financial deficit, which, in April 1946, stood at £919.17s.0d. And yet, the club had survived. Both course and clubhouse were intact. Major Kitchin, Secretary since 1927, had kept the promise he made to the estate in 1943: "Please do not worry about this place. I will keep it going somehow."

Arthur Robins, West of England Open Champion, c. 1950.

CHAPTER 8

Post-war Problems, 1948–1957

AT THE END of the Second World War the club took stock of its situation. There were eight staff working on the course, comprising green-keeper, tractor driver and six boys who were later replaced by men, though not always as many as six. In the clubhouse were the Steward and his wife. Membership had declined to 116 men and 75 ladies, a decline that inevitably led to a reduced income. Part of the course had been requisitioned by the military and the remainder had suffered through unavoidable lack of maintenance. These problems had to be addressed.

FEES & SUBSCRIPTIONS

A start was made on improving finances by adjusting the level of entrance fees, subscriptions and green fees. The entrance fee of five guineas was suspended in July 1947, when the membership was about two hundred, in the hope of encouraging new members, especially younger ones. In the following year, however, it was re-established at the lower rate of three guineas.

In 1944 the subscription rates were as follows:

FULL		COUNTRY	
Men	Ladies	Men	Ladies
From 1 April 1923			
£4.4s.0d.	£3.3s.0d.	£3.3s.0d.	£2.2s.0d.
Members joining after 14 August 1926			
£5.5s.0d.	£4.4s.0d.	£4.4s.0d.	£3.3s.0d.
Members joining after 5 December 1936			
£5.10s.6d.	£4.10s.6d.	£4.4s.0d.	£3.3s.0d.

In 1945 these annual subscriptions were raised by 10s.6d.

When Commander Bourne from Mullion became Secretary in 1944, he quickly tackled the scale of green fees that had remained virtually unchanged for the previous twenty years. He extended the summer season from April to September, instead of June to September, and introduced new scales as follows:

	Month	Week	Day	After 1 p.m.
Summer	£3.15s.0d.	£1.10s.0d.	6s.0d.	4s.0d.
Winter	£3.0s.0d.	£1.5s.0d.	5s.0d.	3s.0d.

In an effort to attract visitors he had leaflets printed and distributed to the local hotels and to the town council, in which it was stated:

"This club has nearly overcome its post-war difficulties and it is confidently anticipated that the course this year will be up to pre-war standard and that previous difficulties of keeping down the 'rough' will be overcome. It is regarded as one of the most picturesque in Devon. Visitors would like to know that buses from the town run every fifteen minutes and stop three hundred yards from the clubhouse. Green fees are still very moderate."

The club received £703 from the government for "unavoidable depreciation" during the war. No claim could be made for the reinstatement of the nine-hole relief course as the club had decided to abandon it. Initially a contractor was used to return to some order the holes occupied by the army but later, for the sake of economy, the club's own staff were used. A restricted budget meant that the work went ahead piecemeal. About 20 acres required intensive treatment but these were split into 5-acre parcels so that both the success and the cost of the work could be monitored. It was the classic problem: money was short, but without expenditure neither members nor visitors would be attracted in sufficient numbers to improve the financial situation. It was not a short-term difficulty. Well into the 1950s the club had to be subsidised, sometimes to the tune of £1000 annually. Not surprisingly, the estate came to look on the club as "rather an expensive luxury".

Despite its own problems the club was prepared to help others. Assistance continued to be given to Exeter Golf Club. At the end of the war the Exeter club had requested the concession of reduced green fees – half the daily and weekly rates – for its members while the new nine holes, which would complete their course, were being constructed.

COURSE TREATMENT

In March 1946 a visit of inspection was made by the chief advisory officer of the Board of Greenkeeping Research, based at Bingley in Yorkshire. This was at the request of the Secretary, Commander Bourne, who felt that the club should take advantage of the Board's spring tour of the courses in the West Country; the Board would then have first-hand experience of local conditions regarding soil, grass, weeds and turf if consulted in the future.

Certain areas required attention. The turf on the greens, being somewhat matted, needed frequent hollow-tined forking. Weeds on the greens were mostly water chickweed, pearlwort, starweeds and Yorkshire Fog. Fairy rings were also visible. On the fairways weeds were again the main problem. Scarifying was the suggested remedy, together with the application of a new weed-killer, Agroxone. The club agreed to take part in a trial of this and a sample was sent down from Yorkshire. Advice was also given on fertiliser dressings, the one of choice being made up as follows:

20 parts sulphate of ammonia
50 parts super-phosphate
15 parts sulphate of iron
15 parts dried blood

Dried blood was reckoned to have "a more lasting effect on the turf". For the visit and report the club paid £12.7s.6d.

New Machinery

Commander Bourne took care that the suggestions were acted upon. For the weeds a Sisis rake was bought, similar to a Springbok rake but on wheels, "a great saver of time and labour". A Sisis turf-aerator was also purchased. This was a spiking machine and did not eliminate the necessity for hollow-tined forking on the greens as it did not penetrate deeply enough. The cost of both these machines was £28. A turf nursery was also established. In 1947 a distributor, a spiked harrow (for the fairways) and a rotary soil screen were purchased for £75. The reserve tractor, a 1937 Pattisson Bedford, was sold to Sidmouth Golf Club for £275. Its replacement was an Allis Chalmers tractor costing £280. In the following year, 1948, the sale of the three-cut scythe and the two 18-inch mowers supplied the funds for the purchase of a spiked roller. Throughout the fifties sand for the course was obtained through the estate, by permit, from the beach at Exmouth on what appears to have been an annual basis. The amount was either 25 or 50 tons.

Controlling the Rough

The state of the rough was another problem. In the summer of 1947, unbeknown to the Secretary, a deputation from the members called on the estate's Land Agent, Captain Maynard, to make two complaints, one of which concerned the rough. It was held to be too dense. The high heather and ground gorse ensured that it was well nigh impossible to recover a ball, however well marked. The continual search for balls made the game tedious. The Secretary laid the blame for this state of affairs firmly on "the severe petrol restrictions applied to the club". The "meagre allowance" meant that only the fairways could be cut. Even then he had on occasion been driven to appeal to members to donate the odd gallon, which they had done, and he had also bought any unwanted allowances from them.

For the cutting of the rough they were dependent on a local farmer who made up a sizeable hay-rick from it, at the side of the 6th hole, but naturally only did it at his own convenience. Petrol rationing was abolished at the end of the 1940s but the practice of the farmer cutting the

The 7th hole, 1950s.

rough continued as late as 1955. To tame the gorse, there was talk of bringing down a "gorse extractor" owned by Lord Clinton and kept in North Devon, but this does not seem to have happened.

The gorse was also a cause of concern to local homeowners. In about 1950 there was a fire in the area behind and around the 18th green, spreading down to the cliff path. The estate's forestry department then cleared the ground to provide a firebreak in front of nearby houses. In 1957 a resident wrote again to the club, citing the risks of "the untamed jungle" which had been allowed to grow back and urging further action, which was presumably undertaken.

Investment Bears Fruit

The estate continued to invest in the club. In 1949 a great improvement was effected – the provision of an adequate water supply to the greens. Although the normal flow of water to the ram (a machine for forcing by pressure) was over 500 gallons an hour, only about 50 gallons were collected for use owing to the limitations of the existing system. After some research a T.V.O. (tractor vaporising oil) engine and a suitable pump were bought from the engineering firm of Marcus Hodges of Exeter at a cost of £150, plus another £50 for a brick hut to house the machinery. Although the club at this time was running at a loss, the capital outlay was held to be justified. As the Secretary, Colonel Honeyman, wrote:

"We have a reputation of having a fine course, which is attracting many people. With the assurance of having first-class greens, whatever the weather, we will derive more income and the course will be unrivalled in this part of the country."

Looking further ahead, the Ransome motor mower (which could not be used in the war years because petrol was not allowed for it) was replaced in 1956. The estate gave the committee the choice of buying either a Green 17-inch rough-cut Two-Stroke at £67.17s.5d or a Ransome 18-inch mower at £63.18s.4d.

By 1950 the work done on regenerating the links after the war years was beginning to bear fruit. In the summer of that year green fees reached a record level of £1600, exceeding by £200 the 1949 total. The closing down of Exmouth Golf Club at this time also brought thirty new members to East Devon, including Harry Stocker and George Peaker, who were to make major contributions to the club in the future.

Boundary Disputes

All these advances had to be protected in the way that had been done in the past. The course was still surrounded by farmland and, on occasion, the farmers did not consider its interests. Sometimes, it was a matter of boundaries. On the 6th, for example, the cultivated field to the east had gradually been allowed to encroach upon the fairway during the war. This not only changed the shape of the fairway but made an out-of-bounds demarcation more difficult. This dispute was settled amicably in 1948.

Another more definite encroachment occurred two years later when a fence was removed along the western edge of the 7th fairway and the area ploughed up. Even more golf course land was then used for the passage of the farmer's vehicles. Prompt action by the Secretary in requesting the estate to speak to its tenant once again brought the incident to a satisfactory conclusion.

These two examples explain why it was necessary to have the boundaries of the course legally recognised. In 1954 the estate agreed certain "amendments" (unspecified) with Devon County Council which were then assimilated into a six-inch Ordnance Map and agreed by both parties to be the correct position in 1956.

Trespassers on Course

Trespassers were another matter. Various Secretaries in the post-war period noted that the number of people walking over the course was increasing, though in general activity was limited to the rights of way. There was, however, one persistent case of trespass in 1950–51 involving a local resident who, despite warnings, continued to walk at will, accompanied by his two dogs. The following, written by a member, describes what was happening.

"I played a ball from the top of the bank up to the 17th green which went into the bank on the left at the foot of the green. Two black dogs, which were accompanied by their owner promptly left him and retrieved the ball and took it to him, which he put into his pocket. When I got to the bottom of the hill I went up to him and accused him of having my ball, a Dunlop 65, which he produced and said that he was well aware that it was my ball and that he was sorry. I told him that I would report the matter".

The Secretary then wrote to remind the trespasser that balls found on the course "were the property of the proprietor". A similar case had come before the High Court in 1949, when judgement was found in favour of the club and the offender was prosecuted for larceny. This particular offender, however, was undeterred and it was not until several months later when, faced with the threat of an injunction by the estate's solicitors, he stopped his illegal activity.

CHAPTER 9

The Years 1958–1963

AFTER THE painting of the outside of both the clubhouse and golf cottage in 1958, the following year saw a comprehensive overhaul of the internal facilities of the clubhouse at a cost of £3000. The main work involved the provision of a new kitchen and the updating of the Steward's living quarters, including the staircase to the flat. A new bar was created with its own lighting, shelving, beer-store and washing-up area.

The sum of £200 was spent on installing night-storage heating and for a further £100 the Secretary's office was converted into an extension of the men's locker room. Numerous small repairs, including the modernisation of gas and electric fittings, were also undertaken. Not surprisingly, considering that the building was almost sixty years old, part of the roof had to be renailed and two chimney stacks taken down. The one serving the Steward's sitting room fireplace was rebuilt, for which Carters charged £42.

Scrub Clearance

In March 1959 the estate became concerned about a perennial problem affecting the course – rabbits! It was felt that one solution, not previously tried, was to destroy the creatures' habitat by clearing scrub from certain areas, cutting 'rides' through the gorse and bulldozing a number of banks and the largest of the warrens. The work envisaged qualified for a grant under the provisions of the Pests Act of 1954, subject to inspection by a local official from the Ministry of Agriculture. Several firms were asked to tender and the successful bid came from Grange Plant Ltd of Honiton.

At the completion of the scheme about four acres of scrub had been destroyed and some seventeen differing lengths of bank levelled, the longest stretch being 250 yards. Eighteen "rides", each 2 feet wide, had been created. Three of them measured 175 yards. These "rides", which could be used on horseback or on foot, were made to give access to the densest parts of the vegetation in order to make the hunting down of rabbits easier. An added advantage might well have been that stray golf balls were easier to find! The work – the bill for which was £459 – must have radically altered the landscape and "opened out" the course to a degree which would have surprised the original architect. Today the remains of some of the banks can still be seen.

Perhaps understandably, such a major upheaval was not accomplished without some difficulties. Firstly, it took a long time. Begun in August 1959, the work was not completed until October 1960. Secondly, the treated areas were left in a state that would be difficult to maintain. The stony ground was so uneven that it would be impossible to use a reaper and the new Secretary, L. R. Allen, expressed his worries that "maintenance would place a burden on our resources such as few golf clubs are called upon to bear". So the estate responded by calling in another contractor to rotavate the most difficult areas and to level them sufficiently for grass seed to be put down.

In an effort to follow up this major anti-rabbit drive, the estate organised a shoot over the course in the winter of 1961. The Secretary was "delighted" about the rabbits and cheerfully wrote:

"We have many who are members of the club but I will keep them out of the way and I wish you all the luck in the world with the rest. We seldom see the four footed ones, but judging by scratch marks and droppings they have increased very considerably in the last twelve months."

Two years later the ritual had to be repeated after an anguished letter from the Secretary, in which the words "rabbits" and "menace" appeared in close proximity!

"It is now quite possible to lose a ball on the fairway. In my humble opinion the only way to get them in a big way is to go out in the very early morning or shoot them at night by car headlights. Incidentally, poachers have done the latter but the trouble is that they drive over the greens and spoil them. They have been caught by the police."

MORE IMPROVEMENTS

Mr L. R. Allen, who had been appointed in July 1960 on the death of Commander Bourne, was to prove energetic and forceful. Under his guidance the club moved forward with growing confidence, which, after some years, led it into a new era of self-government. Immediately after taking on his duties Allen identified four courses of necessary action:

1. The replacement of the existing tractor. This was achieved almost immediately at a cost of £475.

2. An extension to the existing trolley shed. This too was put in hand in a matter of weeks. An increase in membership made the extension desirable even though, as we have seen, it was only five years since a new trolley shed had been built at the back of the Professional's shop. The improvement was also linked to a proposed rise in subscriptions. In October 1960, therefore, the architect, Antony Lamb of Ottery St Mary, produced a design for a cedar-wood shed, 434 square feet in area. This was to be attached to the north wall of the existing building. The two windows in this wall were to remain since the lean-to roof of the extension would have perspex sections in it to admit light to them. The roof was to be made of asbestos cement sheeting coloured to match the roof tiles of the main building. The shed would be provided with sliding doors.

The plan did not meet with total approval. Members were dissatisfied with the internal arrangements which, they felt, perpetuated a major disadvantage of the existing accommodation. Careless golfers, ignoring the hooks provided, left their trolleys on the central floor space for others to fall over. The Secretary's answer was to divide the space into five bays 6 feet in width, each with its own entrance secured by a roller shutter. This, he hoped, would reduce congestion for the 64 men and 43 ladies seeking storage for their trolleys. He got his way. The firm of E. W. Bastin carried out the work, which was completed in April 1961, for the sum of £622.15.0d.

3. The repair of the 200-yard stretch between Northview Road and Links Road. Allen may not have known that in July 1959 the estate had asked the Budleigh Salterton Urban District Council to undertake the making up of the road and to maintain it in the future. It appears that the request was refused. Patchwork repairs were undertaken at intervals but the weight of lorries delivering goods to the clubhouse – particularly beer lorries! – quickly undid the good work. Members naturally complained of having to negotiate potholes and so at the end of 1961 the estate paid £170 to have this section of road laid with tarmacadam.

In the summer of the same year, while there was heavy machinery on the course dealing with the scrub, the opportunity was taken to enlarge the car park. Defined by posts and rails, the new space, alongside that already available, allowed for a second line of cars, "a real necessity" in the summer months according to the Secretary. In these two ways access to the club was considerably improved.

4. The renewal of the water pipeline feeding the reservoir. This matter was more slowly resolved even though it was potentially serious since the malfunction would quickly have had a detrimental effect on the course, particularly the greens, which would cause, in all probability, a drop in revenue. However, it was not until February 1963 that the estate agreed to carry out the work.

The delay may have been because the estate was being asked to meet a number of other requirements for the course and clubhouse during 1961 and 1962 over and above those already itemised. They may be summarised as follows:

- 50 field drain pipes to replace old and broken ones.
- 10 tons of lime to be put down on gorse clearings.
- 100 tons of bunker sand from Blackhill Quarries.
- 20 tons sea sand from Exmouth – several requests.
- Purchase of an Allman Speedispray, Sisis

Rotorake and a Versatile Broadcaster. The cost for the three was £150.

- Maintenance of existing machinery – at least £140.
- Seats at tees on all the holes.
- Drainage of valley on the 17th hole.
- Tree planting in gaps caused by gales – 1000 trees were requested.
- 80 tons of topsoil, used in compost for the greens and in divotting. The Land Agent asked if 15 tons would suffice. At 15s. a ton topsoil was expensive and difficult to obtain.

The Secretary was adamant: "The course is now getting a great deal of wear. Our membership has almost doubled and Green Fees are a good deal higher. One could economise by reducing the fairway divotting but this is far from ideal and members are so keen on having the course in good condition that they have again volunteered to do the job themselves without the ground staff and I would be very reluctant to discourage them."

In contrast to the decision made over the trolley-shed extension Allen did not, in this instance, get his way. It was decided to "stand over" the whole matter of fulfilling the list of requirements submitted by the Club.

CLUB OBTAINS LEASE

For most of the 1950s East Devon operated at a loss, the worst year being 1949–50, when the deficit stood at £1435. However, towards the end of the decade matters improved to the extent that between 1958 and 1961 a profit of about £3000 was generated for, and handed over to, the estate. It was therefore not necessarily available to fund the improvements requested during 1961 and 1962 and listed above.

Although to some this might seem unfair, the estate was conscious that there had been a continuous record of losses at the club prior to 1950, requiring substantial subsidy by the estate. The Land Agent felt that the estate should receive the profit generated by the club in lieu of rent. The club had never paid rent for the course and premises, though a nominal rent did appear in the accounts.

At a meeting with the Secretary in March 1962 the Land Agent suggested that the club might take a lease and run its own affairs. Allen replied that he thought the members would be "quite satisfied" to do this. The proposal would help to increase "club spirit" and a "sense of loyalty", which were often absent in a proprietary club. Decision-making would be speeded up and members, through their committee, would have the final say in the allocation of funds for specific projects.

By June a draft lease had been drawn up and negotiations began on the details of its terms. The Secretary, the Captain and a sub-committee, formed for the purpose, represented the club. One main concern for members was the prospect of having to undertake capital works – such as course reconstruction – at the start of the new venture. Finances might be strained just as the club was beginning to feel its way. The estate was pressed to undertake certain work so that the newly self-governing club could be launched with "a clean slate". Discussions also centred on the amount of the future annual rent and the number of years for which the lease would run.

By November 1963, at the end of almost eighteen months of proposals and counter-proposals, the club had achieved many of its goals. The estate undertook:

1. To install the new pipeline on the 17th. Brittons of Tiverton did the work for £172.

2. To reconstruct the 14th, 15th and 16th holes. The firm of Franks Harris of Guildford laid out the greens between Easter and October 1964 at a cost of £1830.

"We are very pleased with the layout" wrote the Secretary, "and we are confident that in two years time the three virtually new holes will be of notable value to the Course."

3. To bring Chine Cottage (the Head Greenkeeper's house) up to modern standards. Carters charged £1083 to do this.

4. To repair the men's locker room floor. The bill was £210.4s.0d.

In recognition of this expenditure the club gave

up its demand to retain the accumulated profits.

The lease – which was a full repairing one – was due to come into effect on 25 March 1964 and indeed the club did assume control of its own affairs at that date. However, the legalities were not completed, and the leases exchanged, until over a year later. The term of the lease was for 20 years 9 months. For the first three years the annual rent was £750, rising to £900 for the subsequent four years. Thereafter it was to be renegotiated.

One reason for the delay in finalising the change-over was the great deal of discussion that went on about – rabbits! The Secretary specifically asked that a clause be inserted for dealing with them. The land included in the lease covered 142.96 acres and the club was given permission to shoot rabbits over that area after agreement with the farmer at Littleham who had the shooting rights over a wide stretch of countryside which included the course.

East Devon was to be a private members' club. Four trustees were appointed. Lord Clinton was asked "to do us the honour of remaining our President". His acceptance was declared to be "most popular with the whole of the Club". In this way the desire for self-regulation, which had been building among members for several years, was fulfilled. In 1964 the club was both profitable and solvent. It was now up to those willing to take on the role to use these twin advantages to develop a vibrant and flourishing Golf Club.

The Secretary – as so often in the past – had the last word. "I am sure the change will be for the good of the Club, but less sure it will be so good for me! There is just as much politics here as there is in Westminster."

The old 12th green, c.1960

CHAPTER 10

The Sixties and Seventies

THE CLUB celebrated its new-formed freedom by going on a spending-spree which was funded, initially at least, by the generosity of the estate. It was prepared to pay for new machinery for the course, new furniture for the clubhouse and for equipment over £10 in value which had a life of more than two years. Furnishings, such as curtains and floor-coverings, were not included and neither was any major development, such as an extension to the building.

Between November 1964 and November 1965 approximately £2000 was spent on course machinery, including a turf piercer, a turf shredder, a 3-unit gang mower and an elm roller for the greens.

Yet, as the Secretary stated, the expense was justifiable. "The question of a clubhouse extension will arise very soon and, with present cost of labour, more mechanisation on the course is a serious consideration."

The estate's financial involvement meant that its Land Agent could be assured, "We are comfortably making ends meet." It may have been a mistake. In early 1966 the estate declined to pay for any more course machinery, including the two Atco 4-stroke green machines – at £95 each – and a new tractor already delivered. The Allis Chalmers E.D. 40 (Diesel) tractor was expensive. Complete with golf course wheels and front-end loader it cost £943. The club was undeterred. In May it bought a Rutland 3 1/2 ton tipping trailer, priced £160.

At this point the updating process was complete. For the next few years the only purchases were a Flymo Professional machine at £44 in 1967 to replace the Rough Cut machines worn out after eight years' service, a Sisis Roto-rake at £100 in 1971, a Ransome Surtees 20 inches greens mower and another Flymo was purchased in 1972.

Course Management

The pattern of care continued as it had done in the past. The greens still required specialist treatment, the grass on the fairways still had to be encouraged to grow and weeds had to be eliminated. The rhythm of the seasons still largely dictated what could and could not be done. For detailed reports on the health of the course the club continued to rely on the Turf Research Institute. In the sixties the dressings of choice for the greens were Verdesan, Lornox and nitro-chalk. The fairways were sprayed with Cornox G. On one occasion four tons of Ground Rock Phosphate were worked in because a test on soil samples had shown a severe deficiency in phosphate. The cost was £48. Hoof and horn meal – again, recommended by the Institute – was added to a general fertiliser such as Co-Fertil that cost £64 for 10 tons. Dried blood, purchased at £3 per cwt, was also used.

Tee Rebuilding

In 1974 a new tee was built and turfed at the 1st hole. In 1976 the committee decided on a programme of tee rebuilding in the knowledge that this might well take three years. In 1975 a "starter shelter" was bought in memory of Geoffrey Powell, who had made such a substantial financial contribution to the purchase of the Automatic Irrigation System. How many members over the years, either waiting to tee off or starting competitions, must have been glad of its protection!

It was not always the case of "off with the old and on with the new". An endearing – and enduring – feature of the course was the series of huts situated at points all across it. Some may well have been the original ones inherited from the Budleigh Salterton Golf Club in 1902. Whatever their vintage they were carefully repaired and repainted. In 1966 they stood at the 5th, 8th, 10th, 13th and 15th holes. A new one, costing £36.6s.0d. from Carters, was bought for the 17th tee.

Improving the Bunkers...

There was a good deal of dissatisfaction with the state of the bunkers in the seventies. In 1974 a resolution was passed in committee: "A long term policy is needed in our bunkers, considered one of our poor features." Two years later they were still considered to be in "bad condition". In that year the bunker on the 16th was made G.U.R. until such time as it could be redesigned. The problem was that strong winds continually blew the sand away.

A more widespread difficulty was drainage. A plan was evolved, also in 1976, for "deep digging" all the bunkers in order to remove the old Blackhill Quarry sand down to the pebbles. When this was done, however, there was found to be only about one inch of the old red sand atop stones, rubble and sometimes clay, so the bunkers were refilled.

The choice of sand itself was not a straightforward matter. In the 1960s sharp sand from the ECC Quarries and silver sand from Allenvale Quarries were experimented with. In the 1970s Leamoor sand was tried. The last, at £3 per ton, was more expensive than Exmouth sand at £1 per ton. But sea sand from Exmouth was becoming difficult to obtain since there were restrictions on its removal. However, with the help of the estate, a quantity was obtained although it required cleaning, having come from the huts behind the Maer. In 1976 the club managed to build up a stockpile. The Captain reported: "We should now have enough for about three years and a club production of 'The Desert Song'!"

In 1979 the overriding feeling was still that the bunkers were "the worst feature of the course" and so the solution of "deep digging" was resurrected. The Golf Architect Mr Hamilton Stutt, asked to make an inspection, reported in 1980 although it was not until 1981 that a start was made on his proposals. The bases of the bunkers were then reconstructed. Land drains were placed beneath draining stones, on top of which was a 4-inch layer of sand. Surface water was taken to soakaways. Top filling was to be of Exmouth sand. Seven bunkers were treated in this way. In order of priority they were:

15th – right and left greenside
2nd – right greenside
11th – right greenside
13th – right greenside
10th – right front greenside
1st – left side under the bank
short of the green.

Only the first four were given "the full Hamilton Stutt treatment". On the 10th, and in particular on the 1st, which the ladies had complained about, it was felt that the problem lay in balls getting right under the face of the bunker, and so the sand and soil were relevelled in these two bunkers to give a gentler slope up to the face. The work was completed by the end of 1980.

... and the Greens

In 1973 the club bought a Ransome-Hahn Triplex Mower for use on the greens. Although expensive, mechanisation was seen as the answer to the staff shortages then being experienced. The effect was as expected – all the greens could be cut in three and a half hours. Since the Turf Advisory Institute had advised more frequent cutting, the greens were mowed four times a week in the peak growing season. A second-hand roller was acquired from the Cricket Club and given an overhaul and new motor, although there were fears that it might prove too heavy.

Again, on the advice of the Institute, hollow tining was a regular part of the care of the greens, undertaken after scarifying. In some years the Club bought in this service because its own equipment could not do such a thorough job. It was expensive. The hire of a Greensaire machine and operator cost £216 in 1975.

By 1979, when Chipmans carried out the work, the price had risen to £399 and by 1981 it was £475. Sand and "slitting" were follow-up tasks for the club's own staff. When the greens' soil showed signs of turning acidic they were dressed with carbonnade of lime – again on the instructions of the Board of Greenkeeping Research.

A New Path

In early 1974 excess wear around the 7th green was causing concern. Making a path from the green through the bushes by the shed to the 8th tee solved the problem. A bunker was then built on the left edge of the green so that players would have to take their trolleys to the left of it. By the summer this new path was "being used and liked". In 1980 only wide-wheeled trolleys were allowed on to the course.

Practice Ground

In 1965 the Secretary, L. R. Allen, asked the estate's permission to clear the heather to the north of the 1st fairway, arguing that "the construction of a good practice course would considerably add to our amenities". The following year the "Swipe" machine, borrowed from the estate, and an excavator worked for a week to clear the gorse from the specified area. Several trees were also removed. By the end of the year a newly constructed tee was ready to turf. Some years later, two more tees were made for driving practice and another two for irons. The whole area was then "tidied up".

In 1975 the construction of a par 3 hole to the right of the 18th fairway was proposed. It was to be properly laid out with tee, bunkers, apron and green. Although welcome as a new facility, the plan was postponed as it was thought "better to concentrate [funds] on maintaining the existing facilities to a good standard rather than spreading them on new projects". The scheme was eventually implemented in January 1979. By September, water had been laid on and the green was ready for seeding.

Rabbits and Trespassers

As in past years, the course, on which so much thought and effort were lavished, had to be shielded from possible damage from certain quarters. Rabbits continued to be a nuisance – particularly, for some reason, in 1964! The "County Pest Officer" was consulted, the "Rabbit Society" appealed to but, in the end, they resorted to tried and tested methods -"the gun, ferreting and lurchers and nets".

Trespassing, too, was an area of course management that needed constant vigilance. In 1964 a notice was put at the entrance to the footpath from Castle Lane beside the 6th green, banning vehicles from the track. A year later a padlocked gate was put up at the same point. In 1971 a noticeboard ("EDGC Private") was erected by the reservoir at the 15th, another point of access on to the fairways. A similar notice was placed near the 5th tee "to try and stop pedestrians crossing the course". Beside the 3rd tee was placed the warning: "Members only – no right of way." How effective these measures were is not known.

Restricting Use

To prevent overcrowding on, and excessive use of, the course the committee agreed in September 1972 that no societies should be allowed to play between mid-July and mid-September and that visitors with County Cards should also be banned during the same period.

Cliff Erosion

In December 1979 the club again faced a recurring problem in its history – cliff erosion. Once again the affected area was the 16th hole, where the cliff path had to be brought in to the edge of the gorse over a stretch of 135 metres. In this instance the 17th hole was also affected. Here the path was moved 3 metres inland over a 55-metre length. The move affected the old back tee, part of which was lost, making it necessary to extend the tee forward. The club hoped that an 8-feet high fence would be erected to screen the course but, in the event, had to settle for one of 6 feet.

Return of the Pheasants

In 1979 it was decided to put pheasants back on the course. Older members could recall seeing as many as twenty during a round. One of the members never forgot seeing "a hen hustle her brood of fifteen chicks from the 3rd green and turn, with head and wings lowered, to defend

Text continues on page 81...

The 13th Green, c.1905. The 14th green can be seen top right.

Charles Pine-Coffin "drives in" on Opening Day on 31st March,1902.

The 1st Green, c. 1903 (now on the 3rd Fairway).
Members relaxing outside the Clubhouse in the 1930s.

The Clubhouse , professional's shop and 'bicycle shed', c. 1905.
The Clubhouse in 1972, after the first extension.

Palairet Memorial Trophy Winners 1968 and 1969: Back row l to r: F Kemp, H A Trapnell, C E Marker, K L Trott, R W T Blake, S F Allitt, G H Law; Front row J H Trapnell, J H Wyllie, R G L Benzie, W A Kain.

Men's Palairet Memorial Trophy Winners 1987: Back row l to r: B Devetta, R Martin, M Pagliero, G Baker, A Pelosi, P Newcombe, G Page; Front row: R Benzie, R Blake, R Greenaway, A Sage, A Richards.

Katie Tebbet as English stroke play champion.

Paul with his trophies in 1986.

Palairet Memorial Winners 2000.Back row: R Martin, B Spurrier, K J Harper, R J Humphrey, P W Webber, P M Newcombe, B W Stevens; Front row, G J Harper, J P Smith, D Sharp, MBE, T Heard, (Captain), G T Page, D M Crookall. Below: The Centenary Committee: Back row l to r: B Smith, D Watson, R Burley, R Greenaway (Centenary Captain), J Price; Front row: J Miller (Centenary Lady Captain), A M R Miller (Chairman), Kathleen Harland (Centenary History Author).

Ladies Still Cup 1992. Back row: E Ford, J Bell, S Joll, K Tebbet, E Hunt; Front row, J Miller, M Onley (Captain), M Christie.

Aerial view of the course with Budleigh Salterton in the background.

Ladies Past Captains: Back row l to r: H Greenaway, J Hall, T Philp, V Freeman, M Whitehead, M Tye, J Halton, J Benzie, S Wild, L. Caldwell; Front row: M Onley, G Phipps-Turnbull, B Knight, J Miller, J Berry, M Edwards, N Orange, P Powell. Not in photo D. Oag, A. Smith, H. Coton, P. Hayes,S. Nankivell.
Below: Mens Past Captains: Back row l to r: T Heard, D Watson, N Griffin, P Lilley, J Saul, A M R Miller, R Lankester; Front row: A Sage, G Young, R Benzie, R Greenaway, G Baker, M Yates. Not in photograph: J MacCormick, R Blake, A Oag.

The Clubhouse with the 17th Green in the foreground: High Peak and Sidmouth Vale beyond.

The 1st Green in April.

The 8th Green and the Exe Estuary.

The 2nd Green.

Part of the Practice Putting Green.

The world's foremost golf course artist, Graeme Baxter, at work on the Centenary Painting for East Devon Golf Club.

Max Faulkner demonstrates his skills to members in August 1977.

"Hannah" with some of the 38,000 golf balls she has found at East Devon since 1993.

1930's caricatures from the "Picture Match" Trophy played for annually against Sidmouth Golf Club.

Scratch Silver Medal dating from 1908.

The Pine-Coffin Cup and The Rolle Cup, both presented in 1902.

The 10th "one of the nicest Par Three's I have ever seen" – Graeme Baxter.

The 10th Green in August.

Heather on the 13th.

The 11th Green.

Buttercups and blossom on 5th Fairway.

The 4th Green with part of the 9th Fairway in the background.

The Par Five 6th Green in August.
The left hand Bunker at the 6th.

Newly planted trees on the 7th Fairway.

Wild flowers and heather in August with the 9th Green beyond.

"Early purple"orchid on the 7th Fairway.
Below: Heather around the 3rd Green.

The 12th Green in early Spring.

The 12th Green a few months later.

The 7th Green in late April.

The 18th Green with recently planted Rhododendron.

"The View"
Below: The 18th Green.

... *continued from page 64*

them". In an effort then to recreate those days, twelve fully grown birds were introduced to a semi-enclosed area between the 12th and 17th and encouraged to settle. Members were asked to stay away from the area and reminded that, since the pheasant was the club mascot, it was, therefore, "sacred" and was allowed "the freedom of the course". The local fox population, however, may not have been aware of this ruling!

The Palairet Trophy

The late 1960s and early 1970s were very successful years for the club's Palairet Teams, which won the coveted trophy four years in succession, from 1969 through to 1971. (*See Colour Section photo on page 68.*)

Standard Scratch

In 1977 it was agreed that the Standard Scratch should be raised to 70. This was to be achieved by adding 41 yards at the 12th (par 5), 16 yards at the 13th and 10 yards each at the 16th and 17th. The total yardage of the course was then 6217 yards. At the same time the Stroke Index was altered to read 4 at the 14th and 6 at the 17th.

The First Extension

The idea of extending the clubhouse was raised in committee in 1965. Total membership was 630. Because of a lack of accommodation, a limit to full membership had been set at 275 men and 110 ladies. However, it was not until March 1971 that the members, at an EGM, authorised the committee to proceed with the outline plan as drawn up by the architect, Mr Bradshaw.

One objective was to increase the area of the lounge and dining room. This was achieved by "pushing out" the south wall of the building to enclose what had been the veranda. The line of the new wall ran from just behind the door leading from the Ladies Lounge – now the Pheasant Room – to the outside. Sliding patio doors and picture windows forming almost the entire length of the new wall ensured that a splendid view could be enjoyed over the 18th fairway to the cliffs and sea beyond. The sunny, southerly aspect made some shade a necessity so overhead blinds of the 'Dutch type' were fitted, not only along the new extension but also over the window of the Ladies' Lounge. The price for these was £348. *(See Colour Section photo on page 77.)*

A second objective was to provide better changing facilities for the men. A new men's locker room was created by building out from the north wall of the entrance hall, stopping at the line of the existing locker room. A small lobby was created in the north-east corner to give direct access from the area of the Professional's shop and the car park to the changing rooms and thence to the interior of the clubhouse. The cost of new lockers, alterations to existing lockers in the old room and island units for all the locker rooms was about £1100.

The all-male committee made the decisions on the furnishings. In the lounge the Lloyd Loom chairs were resprayed and their cushions recovered. New tables were ordered. New curtains for the large windows cost £350. This area, together with the bar, was painted blue.

Elsewhere, reddish-brown carpet tiles were chosen for the locker rooms, hall and all the ladies' rooms.

Another addition to the clubhouse was an imposing double-door entrance on the west side of the building not far from the flagstaff. That year had also seen the updating of the Professional's shop – with a new door and double plate-glass windows – at a cost of just under £5000. Behind the shop, in the same year, a practice putting green was created in the vicinity of the old 16th green, still much in use today by those waiting to tee-off.

The extension was officially opened by Lord Clinton on 3rd November 1972. In his speech, the Captain, Group Captain Tebboth, remarked that the clubhouse was "no longer the ugly sister of the finest golf course in Devon" yet he was aware that "a small minority" was critical, "painfully surprised that anyone in his right mind could contemplate making any changes whatsoever". On a happier note, however, the work during the alterations had been so well coordinated within the club that, "like the wartime Windmill Theatre, we never closed!"

After this no major building work was undertaken during the 1970s. There was always a realistic awareness that the ability to carry out improvements rested on a healthy financial situation and plenty of attention was directed to that area. Over the years, the club has been fortunate in having so many willing members prepared to give their time and use their expertise in its service.

Every month the finances were looked at by the committee and it frequently had the pleasure, as in 1974, of recording "how well we had kept our expenses down in the running of the Club". So good was the overall position that subscriptions remained unchanged between April 1973 and July 1976. One of the reasons behind the buoyant finances was the rise in green fees.

Green Fees Rise

One reason for the rise was that in April 1973 the club had increased the charge to visitors playing the course by 60 per cent. Green fees rose from £1.25 to £2.00 plus 20p VAT. This was despite the government price freeze then in operation. Its right to do so was challenged by the county's Weights and Measures Inspector and the subsequent hearing was reported in national newspapers. The club argued that, as a private organisation, it could set its own charges, a claim that was upheld by the Department of the Environment. Subsequent comment centred on the likelihood of dearer golf nationwide as a result of the ruling.

Significant Features

The club carried on as before. There was the continuing recognition that East Devon was a club of distinction, a fact that should be reflected in its physical surroundings. In 1977, Honours Boards were purchased at a cost of £530. In 1979, Dan Driver's offer to execute a humorous picture depicting golfing 'types' was accepted. His caricature of incoming Captains – displayed in the clubhouse during their captaincy – was always enjoyed. Thought was given to the correct placing of a collection of old golf clubs given by the widow of the Hon. Mark Rolle at his death in 1907. It was decided to display them in a purpose-made glass case, costing £200, to be positioned in the entrance hall. The club's old feather ball and

Caricatures of personalities in the 1960s.

the gold tee presented some years earlier for use at a Captain's drive-in were placed alongside. A heartening sign of a club pulling together led to the decision, in the same year, to provide a quarterly Newsletter "informing members of items of interest".

Social Events

A popular annual event throughout the sixties was the Club Dinner that was held every December, for men only. It normally attracted about sixty members. In 1965 the meal cost fifteen shillings.

Dances were another feature of social life in the clubhouse and, although they were held only occasionally during this period, they were well supported. In February 1964, ninety-two members enjoyed an evening's dancing for the price of twenty-one shillings! Cocktail parties – at half the cost of a dance – were also enjoyed.

In 1966 an Entertainments Committee was formed with realistic objectives:

"The question of social events, apart from the Captain's Dinner, concerns only a minority of our members but there is an evident desire on the part of these to have some functions during the year. Care should be taken to preserve the reputation of the Club."

Possibly as a result of this initiative, a more formal dinner and film show was organised at the Rosemullion Hotel the following year.

In 1972, the year of the completion of the clubhouse development, the Ladies Captain and Vice-Captain were invited to join the Entertainments Committee. There was the wish to make full use of the new facilities and to offer social events that would appeal to a wide range of members. Friday evenings were proposed as club nights, when the bar would stay open until 10.30 p.m. and some social golf might be organised. The offer to buy a Captain's Chair was also made at this time and accepted.

1972 was a year – and there would be others in the future – when thought was given to the correct dress to be worn by men in the clubhouse. A notice designed "to maintain the dignity of the club" was posted. "Appropriate neckwear with a jacket or sleeved cardigan is to be worn at all times in the dining room and after 6.00 p.m. in the bar and lounge. Open-necked shirts are not permitted at any time."

The increasing popularity of informal dances in the clubhouse led to the purchase, in 1974, of a portable dance floor, bought from Stover Golf Club for £75. This acquisition led to the introduction of dinner dances, which were usually limited to forty persons. In 1974 the cost of such a function was £2 per head! In some years two functions were held, one in the summer and one at Christmas.

One fixture in the social calendar was the outside annual dance held in spring. Venues in the 1970s were the Pavilion and the Imperial Hotel in Exmouth, where anything up to 170 members and guests danced the night away – and all for the price of a £4 ticket!

In the days before satellite television brought live sport to our screens, a film show might be the only chance of viewing a major sporting event. So films of the most recent Open, or of a major American tournament, were quite often shown and were well attended – especially when they were accompanied by a 'tasting' of wine or spirits. Talks on subjects of golfing or general interest were also held.

The first Christmas Draw was held in 1973. Before that there had been a draw every two months. It was a useful source of income for the club at a time when it was seeking to build up reserves after taking over the lease.

The year ended – as might be expected – with a buffet dance. Always described as "very successful", these occasions attracted so many that, towards the end of the 1970s, numbers had to be limited to eighty. At about £2 a head they were good value – though the licence was usually extended only to 12.15 a.m.

The Freehold

In September 1978 there was discussion about the possibility of buying the freehold. Professional advice was taken and, in January 1979, an offer was made, which was rejected. Although the bid was increased in February and again in March it was not enough and in April the estate decided not to sell "at present".

CHAPTER 11

Ladies' Golf

1902 – 1920

The Beginning

On 12th April 1902 Mr Chamier, Land Agent for the Rolle Estate, sent out a notice to the effect that "a General Meeting of Lady Members of East Devon Golf Club" would be held at the clubhouse on 21st April with the purpose of electing a Ladies' Committee and Lady Secretary. There was obviously some interest in this proposal as eighteen ladies attended, together with Mr Chamier and Mr Oliver, the club Secretary. Two of the ladies present were young Miss Oliver, the Secretary's daughter, and Miss Tosswill, whose father had supervised the laying-out of the course.

At a subsequent meeting it was explained that the ladies could attend "general meetings" of the club but had no right to vote. From the start, therefore, it was made clear to them that they were not full members of the club. Without voting rights their influence was lessened. To a great extent the committee of the main club would

Ladies on the 18th, c.1903 (the present 2nd green)

Ladies approaching the original 5th green c.1905. This became the 12th green in 1914.

decide how and when they played golf. The ladies would be able to make their wishes known but might or might not be able to achieve their aims.

Early Organisation

From the eighteen ladies present at the first meeting a committee of six was elected and Mrs Thomas, who chaired the next meeting, accepted the office of Hon. Secretary. She was to serve for eight years. On her retirement in 1910 the ladies arranged "a testimonial" for her and also requested Lord Clinton to make her a life member of the club. It is not known whether this request was granted but if so, she would be the club's first honorary member.

It was not until 1906 that the first Captain, Miss Morant – who was held to be the best player – was elected. Annual General Meetings began in 1902 and continued – with breaks in 1907 and 1908 due to lack of numbers – until 1913, just before the outbreak of the First World War. They were restarted in 1919. It was in the minutes of the AGM of April 1911 that the term "East Devon Ladies Golf Club" was first used.

Ladies' Competitions

Right from the start the founder members were interested in competitive golf. In September 1902 the decision was made to hold a Monthly Medal, with a prize of a silver teaspoon for the winner. These spoons were paid for out of the £7 granted by the men's committee for prizes. (The amount was variable. In 1903 it dropped to £6 but in later years was raised to £10.) At Medal competitions there was also an "optional sweep" of sixpence. In 1913 it was decided that players in the medal competitions should be divided into two sections, "numbers up to and including 20 handicap to be in the first division". At the same time a meeting was arranged with the club Secretary to discuss "some permanent medal tees for the ladies".

The first Open Day dates back to 1902, but the first meeting of which there are details took place in September 1904, held over two days. The first day was devoted to "Ladies Singles, Ladies approach, putting for Men and Ladies" and the second day was taken up with "Ladies foursomes (Bogey) and mixed foursomes (Medal)". In 1905 only nineteen couples took part in spite of

Ladies' and Gentlemen's putting competition, c.1907.

invitations to neighbouring clubs, but this grew to thirty-eight couples the following year. Various members took it in turns to provide the £1 prize money (later raised to thirty shillings).

The Still Cup competition was begun in 1903 and was won by East Devon in 1904.

The First Trophies

It was a Miss Mathieson, a stalwart member in these early days, who, in 1909, presented the first trophy – a Challenge Cup for Mixed Foursomes. This was a popular type of competition. In 1914 the format of her competition was changed to a singles knockout on handicap. A Mathieson Cup is currently played for each autumn by the ladies but may not be the same trophy because the list of winners inscribed on the base starts at 1919. There is thus no definite link to either 1909 or 1914. In 1916 there is mention of a "Captain's Cup" but no reference as to who presented it.

Rules of Play

In 1902 a Handicap Committee, comprising three ladies, was set up and proceeded to revise the handicaps, possibly because the new course was more difficult than the old one near Otterton. Certainly, at one of the first meetings held, the ladies felt that there was a need for tees to be nearer to the fairway, especially at the 1st and the 13th holes. The ladies bogey for the course was agreed at 80 in July 1907.

There are few details available as to scoring and handicaps but in 1913 a bye-law was passed "enabling members with handicaps over 24 to take out a card for reduction of handicap on every day of any week providing they enter their names in the book in the clubhouse before starting out". A similar practice has continued to the present day.

The AGM of April 1909 voted "to try the LGU Handicapping for one year". In 1913 handicaps were limited to 30 "for Club purposes".

A Rare Dispute

The only dispute before 1920 among the ladies concerned one of their number who, despite being warned that her card "was disqualified" went on to sign it for a Medal round and placed it in the box. After much discussion the secretary was asked to write and inform the lady that "a vote of censure" had been passed on her! On the whole, however, the lady golfers were a happy group and even encouraged other ladies to use the clubhouse.

Non-playing Members

In 1911, for example, permission was received from Lord Clinton for members' relatives to become non-playing members. The thinking behind this proposal was outlined by the redoubtable Miss Mathieson: "Many ladies have spoken to me about the hardship of waiting outside the clubhouse for men who are playing, and I thought that as we have large rooms and provide many periodicals, nobody would be inconvenienced if they used our rooms."

For this convenience, non-playing members would pay 5s. per annum. However, Chamier's warning that the development "might evoke a protest from the men" was partially realised the following year when the Lady Secretary had to ask her male counterpart, Mr Whytock, "to refund the subscriptions paid by non-playing lady members, these latter having been declared not to have been properly elected at the General Meeting of the East Devon Golf Club held earlier in the year". As nothing is heard of a continuing dispute the matter must have been settled amicably.

First World War

As might be expected there were few formal meetings or competitions during this time. In 1916 it was agreed that the present Captain, Hon. Secretary and committee should remain in office until the end of the war, and that the Mathieson Cup and the Captain's Cup should not be played for until hostilities had ceased.

A competition was arranged in the same year in aid of the Lord Roberts Memorial Fund for Workshops for Disabled Soldiers and Sailors which was to be held subject to the approval of the General Committee.

The 15th green, c.1907.

There are no minutes of committee meetings between April 1917 and December 1918. The first AGM after the war was held in March 1919. Medal competitions had begun a year earlier.

1920 – 1945

Organisation

The organisation of the ladies' club continued as before. At the beginning of each AGM Lady Clinton was elected President. The committee comprised the Captain, Hon. Secretary and six members elected at the AGM, two of whom had to come from the "Juniors", as the Bronze Division was known.

In 1920 it was decided that the playing year should be altered to begin on 1 January instead of 1 April in order to "fall in line" with the Ladies Golf Union competitions. This decision meant that future AGMs would be held in late November. The names of candidates for the committee were to be submitted by the beginning of the month. In 1939 the post of Vice-Captain was introduced "to deal with 2nd team matches, work in conjunction with the Captain and in the latter's absence to automatically take her place on the committee".

Growing Membership

The election of new members was part of the committee's duties, though all decisions had to be ratified by the "General Committee" of the men's club. A flurry was created in 1922 when a lady member married the Professional. It was discussed at a committee meeting, when a proposal was put forward that "the said member should be asked to resign". It was voted down.

During this time the ladies held two contrasting views on levels of membership. In 1923 they wanted it increased and so wrote to the Secretary, Major Gay, asking "that his Committee would see their way to electing those ladies whose names had been so long on the list". This was done. Possibly, numbers were low. Only twenty-seven members attended the AGM in 1922. However, the building of the 9-hole course – referred to as the ladies' course or the relief course – seems to have brought a change of heart. Perhaps there was a fear of being "swamped". The Ladies' Committee sent up "a strong recommendation" to the men that numbers should not exceed 140. But here, as in other instances, the ladies were not in control of their own destiny. They were told that the men's committee would prefer to use its own discretion "in regulating the inflow of lady members", and a further thirty-two ladies were admitted that year.

In January 1925 the Ladies' Committee walked the new course and suggested some "bye-laws" concerning out of bounds. In May, October and again in February 1926 they raised the matter of the desirability of limiting membership, recommending that only bona fide residents of Budleigh Salterton should be admitted, "as the number was increasing so rapidly". In April play began over the new holes, the LGU having fixed the Standard Scratch at 74. The policy towards membership was finally settled later in the year when the ladies accepted that there should be "no limit" and that the waiting list should be abolished. At this date there were 145 playing lady members and 226 men.

Non-Playing Members

This category of membership did not cause any unease or discussion until 1931, when Major Kitchin decided it might be worthwhile keeping an eye on it. He wrote:

"I forget if there is any limit to non-playing lady members but think there is. This rule was originally started in order to let down lightly some of the original lady members of the club who, although they did not wish to trudge round the course, wished to retain some interest in it. This worked very well until it occurred to certain members that they could give garden parties at the expense of the club servants more easily than at their own homes; it is therefore necessary to keep a watchful eye and not to let everyone automatically, because they have been a member, become a non-playing member."

The 7th, c.1925.

In 1939 ladies' membership stood at 140. At this date the very pleasant ruling was in force, agreed to by the estate, that green fees paid by ladies awaiting membership should be deducted from their first annual subscription.

Relations with Men's Club

In their relations with the men's club the ladies showed persistence in trying to achieve their aims, combined with tact and a realistic approach that showed that they knew where the power lay.

One long-running question concerned "restrictions" placed on the ladies in their use of the "Long Course". These restrictions related to availability and to handicap. For example, in 1921 there was indignation that limits had been imposed without consultation and a letter was sent to the men's committee suggesting that:

1. "ladies 'of senior division' (handicaps 20 and under) be allowed to start at the 1st tee at any time";
2. "ladies being obliged to start at the 13th tee should be allowed to take alternate turns at the 1st tee with those who have not already started";
3. "the ladies' committee should be asked to co-operate with the men's committee in any difficulty connected with the working of the Club, instead of being ignored"!

There was a response to this. Ladies with a handicap of 8 and under were allowed to play from the 1st tee from 1.p.m.

In 1926 a further attempt was made to improve access to the main course. The AGM proposed that:

1. "ladies from 1 April to 30 September be allowed to play on the 18-hole course from 11.a.m.";
2. "ladies be allowed the use of the Long Course from 9.30 – 11.00 a.m. each month for the Ladies' Medal".

Both these requests were refused.

In 1927 the AGM requested that the handicap limit for play on the main course be raised to 12. This too was refused.

In 1928 the AGM asked that the 18-hole course be open to ladies of the correct handicap from 11 a.m. The response was that ladies would be allowed to play from 11.30 a.m. provided they played the first 9 holes on the relief course. The Professional and the Caddie master would be there

Miss M Foster, Devon County Ladies Champion, 1939.

to see that this was done. Presumably, the thinking was that, in all likelihood, the ladies would not be on the main course until after midday.

There matters rested until 1937, when permission was sought for ladies to begin at 10 a.m. for general play. This was agreed to with certain conditions. The handicap limit – now raised to 10 – was kept in force. In addition, the men stipulated that "the courtesy of the Course must at all times be given to male competitors during their monthly competitions". Very sensibly, the Ladies' Committee then put up a notice asking its members "to use their judgement in demanding their rights".

So the policy of polite determination helped the ladies to establish their position and gain acceptance. Some of the men acknowledged this. Major Kitchin wrote: "Ladies are coming more and more to the fore and more and more onto the 1st hole course. They will never be content with the Relief Course."

On the other hand, there was resistance to the ladies gaining any control over the running of the club. When the idea was put forward that ladies of 10 handicap pay the men's subscriptions, Kitchin was doubtful. "Would this automatically give them the right to vote at the A.G.M.s? I am not sure if 'Club Laws' would entitle them to do this. They might be a nuisance!"

He also could not resist passing on "a good story" to Mr Foster, the estate's Land Agent, though in a kindly way because Foster's wife played golf and his daughter, Madge, won the Devon Championship in 1939.

"I was on the 7th green this morning with Wilson doing some levels etc. The entire green is stripped of turf which is laid out all round the place – hundreds of square yards of it.

A lady member got a bit foxed, I suppose, over the new Course and came along up the 7th. She went to Mears (head greenkeeper) and said, 'What on earth are you doing here?'

Mears said, 'Only a little re-levelling, madam.'

The lady said, 'But will the green be fit tomorrow for our Bogey?'!!

Afraid it has aged Mears a bit keeping a straight face!"

The fact that the ladies' position was much better established in 1939 than in 1920 was due not only to their own enthusiasm for the game and desire to contribute but also for financial reasons. It was rumoured that golfing couples avoided East Devon owing to "the restrictions placed on ladies of longer handicaps than 10". It was thought unfair that lady visitors paid the same green fees as men, yet were restricted. Additionally, club numbers were falling, down from the 460 members of a few years earlier to about 400, of whom the men predominated, though only by about 60, which was less than formerly. It was becoming obvious that ladies should have equal access to, and rights on, the course.

Competitions and Medals

Competitions continued to play an important part in the golfing life of the ladies of East Devon. However, even the best-laid plans sometimes go wrong. The March Bogey Competition in 1925 had to be postponed because "the Meet of the Beagles" was due to take place at the clubhouse at the same time!

The main events of the calendar were still the Spring, Autumn and Open meetings. In 1926 permission was granted for these to be played on "the Long Course" provided that they were not held in the busiest months, namely July, August and September.

At the Open, visitors were expected to pay green fees as well as entry fees, though the East Devon ladies protested about it. Two prizes were sometimes awarded in the driving competition, one for the longest drive and one for the aggregate of three drives. Prizes came out of a fund given by the men's club, which stood at £20 in 1939.

Two teams – referred to as the 1st and 2nd – were put out against local clubs, such as Exmouth. The ladies entered the Still Cup, winning in 1926, 1927, 1930 and 1932.

Monthly Medals were played for spoons or badge buttons, usually the former. In the early 1920s, when the club was smaller, prizes were not given in Medals or Bogeys "unless there were 6 entries". In the late 1920s Medals could be played on the 18-hole course only during the autumn and winter. In the busiest months they were 'relegated' to the relief course. This changed in 1933, when play in these competitions was allowed all year round on the main links. It was at this date that the ladies introduced starting time sheets, though they were posted only 24 hours ahead. They were then given to Humphrey, the Caddie master, on the day. Partners were drawn for in all

Still Cup Team 1930.

competitions except Monthly Medals, when the Senior Division and the Junior Division, as they were called, were kept separate. The fear of "big handicap members blocking the course" meant that those on 25 handicaps or over could not start before 10 a.m.

Representation had occasionally to be made about the state of the course. In 1936, for example, the ladies asked "to have new holes cut before the Ladies' Monthly Competition. At present they are cut on Fridays for the men's competitions with the result that ladies get ragged edges to the holes which are impossible to putt into."

In October of the same year they asked for tee mats to be provided for the LGU tees, at a cost of 15s.6d. each. Kitchin, who had just bought nine to replace worn ones on the men's tees, approached the Land Agent to sanction the extra cost. "The tee mats usually last about 3 years. At a pinch we could use the cast-offs from the men's tees. That would mean not buying the whole 18"! Although the club was not doing too well financially at this time, it is clear where his priorities lay!

The ladies took pride in running their events properly and it is noteworthy that in 1937 they decided "that results of all Club Competitions be reported in the press".

Rules Dictated by Men

Some of the rules that were made at this time may seem strange to modern eyes. For instance, any member whose handicap had lapsed played off half the handicap she had last held. In the 1920s the attitude to par was also different. The ladies wrote to the LGU protesting against par "being taken on distance only, irrespective of bad lies and the nature of the ground played over".

There was some change in the allotting of handicaps to the two divisions.

1925	Senior Division	up to and including 20
	Junior Division	over 20
1932	Silver Division	up to and including 18
	Bronze Division	between 19 and 30

It is not known when the terms 'Silver' and 'Bronze' were introduced.

In the matter of rules, as in other areas, the ladies had to take into account the views of the men's committee. In 1926 they were refused permission to print their own "Book of Rules and Bye-Laws", though there was no objection to them printing rules for competitions if first approved by the men. When the 9-hole course was being built it was made clear that "the management of the Ladies' Course and provision of play on it would be under the General Committee".

Directives could be – and were – made which might inhibit the pattern of ladies' play. In 1934 Kitchin requested that Juniors (Bronze Division) would "kindly take out only one Extra Day Card a week on the 18-hole course owing to the wear and tear on the L.G.U. tees". Tactful as ever, the ladies agreed, possibly mindful of the fact that they paid lower subscriptions than the men.

Despite, then, some restrictions on their freedom of action the ladies as a group remained active, enthusiastic and outward looking, qualities that they had retained from the earliest days. They wanted to see the club as a whole develop and improve. Over these years they made repeated requests for "a common room" to be provided.

Delegates were always sent to County and National meetings of the LGU with instructions on how to vote. When, in 1930, they heard that the LGU had approved the principle of playing international matches, their club's name was put on "the subscription list of the Women Golfers' International Match Fund".

One of their last acts, on the outbreak of war, was to decide to have an entry fee for the Bennett Cup, the proceeds of which were to go to the Red Cross Fund.

Thereafter the Minutes fall silent. No meetings were held between April 1940 and November 1945. It is to be presumed that the ladies became engaged in war work and that even those who remained in the area did not have the time or inclination for a great deal of golf.

1945 – 1975

Beginning Again

The striking feature of the immediate post-war years is how long it took for the club to re-establish itself. In 1945 only eight ladies attended the Annual General Meeting and in the following year only one competition was played, for the Bennett Cup. Shortly afterwards Monthly Medals were restarted, though no spoons were given to the winners, presumably because no funds were available. Gradually, the main events returned: the Open in 1947, the Spring meeting in 1948 and the Autumn meeting in 1951. The Still Cup was played for from 1947 onwards.

Numbers did not pick up appreciably throughout the 1950s, the average number present at an AGM being 22. Sometimes there were less than eight ladies competing in Medal and Bogey rounds and, at this time, the minimum number of entries for any competition was fixed as low as four.

However, the effort that this nucleus of members made to support charities associated with the post-war revival programme meant that the fixture list began to fill up. Competitions were organised – for which entry fees were paid – on behalf of King George's Fund for Sailors, the Red Cross, the National Playing Fields Association and the Forces Help Society. The Cathedral Cup was also played for, to raise funds for the repair of Exeter Cathedral. This assistance continued for many years. In addition, annual cheques were sent to the Ladies Golf Union for its International Match Fund.

A further pleasant example of the ladies' generosity occurred in 1954 when they collected £4 for a wedding present for Arthur Robins, the popular Professional. They presented him with a tea service.

Prizes were donated by committee members themselves. In the 1950s one pound for the winner and ten shillings for the runner-up was the norm. In 1954 the men's committee was asked to reinstate the £20 annual prize money given to the ladies before 1939. In these difficult post-war

Ladies on the 7th tee, 1950s.

years, however, the sum was cut to £10. A competition which fell outside the normal prize-giving pattern was that held for the King George's Fund for Sailors. The winner of this normally received either an ashtray, a cigarette lighter or a powder compact from the Association.

The inaugural meeting of the Devon County Veteran Ladies Golf Association was held in 1958. This initiative was supported by the East Devon Ladies, who, over the years, have figured well in the list of prizewinners. In addition, five Lady Captains have been selected from the club. Golf is for all ages, as the lady veterans proved time and time again.

The Committee

For some years after the war, until Mrs Bennett was elected to the post in 1949, the Ladies' Club was without a President. She was to serve in this capacity until 1964. When it is remembered that she was also Honorary Secretary for twenty-five years and had presented the Bennett Cup, her contribution can be seen to have been considerable.

The committee's clear intention was to encourage a club spirit. The second Thursday in each month was designated as a Club Day "for the members to meet and have tea in the Ladies' Room". In an effort to create a pleasant environment successful complaints were made about "the barrels and drink cases" stored in the passageway leading to the ladies' side of the clubhouse. Christmas and New Year "parties" began to be held. These usually involved playing nine holes after which there was tea and a golfing quiz. Sometimes the Secretary of the men's club attended. In a similar vein the ladies were asked to stay behind for tea on Monthly Medal days when the prizes for the previous month's competitions were presented. Two committee members also served on the main club's Social Committee, which was formed in 1961. At this time three ladies were also serving on the County Committee.

The tradition of Captain's Day may go back to 1952, when the then Captain, Miss M. Foster, presented a Jubilee Prize to mark the 50th anniversary of the club's foundation. However, it was an exceptional event as the term "Captain's Prize" was not used again until 1966 and 1967. Captain's Day itself – which became a major event in the calendar – was first held in August 1968, the same year that the Competition Day was changed from Thursdays to Tuesdays. In 1958 a board had been bought for £13 "to record the names of the lady captains". The sum was raised by donations from members.

In the immediate post-war years the position of Vice-Captain was not a regular one. A "Deputy Captain" was appointed temporarily in 1953 because Miss Foster, the Captain, had family commitments. It was not until 1960 that the thirty-three members present at the AGM voted in favour of appointing a Vice-Captain "owing to the greatly increased membership". She was to assist the Captain and "to take the captaincy in the following year". In 1961 the Captain and Vice-Captain became the ladies' representatives on the men's House Committee. Future Vice-Captains were selected by a committee comprising the Captain, the present Vice-Captain and two or more immediate past captains. Lady members' views were taken into consideration.

The post of Hon. Treasurer and Competition Secretary was created in 1972. This was also the year when Miss Stamp ended her eighteen years' run as Secretary. She then undertook the management of the "marriage bureau", through which members found partners for competitions.

Committees encouraged members' opinions. In 1973 the Captain remarked she was glad that the Suggestions Book had been used – since it had last been used in 1938! "Constructive criticism is always valuable to the Committee."

Membership Size

The sixties began well for the Ladies' Club when the Heywood Bowl was won by Pam Powell, "this being the first year the cup had been won by a lady". Growing interest and enthusiasm were revealed by the number attending the AGMs; this increased from 33 in 1960 to 64 in 1969, an average for the sixties being 51. From 1970 to 1975 the average attendance was 71. Permission was received from the men's committee to raise the limit on ladies membership from 100 to 110 in 1964, from 110 to 120 in 1969 and from 120 to 125 in 1973.

Admissions Procedure

There was some disagreement over the admissions procedure. The men's committee wanted the wives of successful candidates for its own club to be given automatic right of entry to the ladies' club, but this was resisted for two reasons. Firstly, it meant that it would be difficult for unmarried ladies to fill any vacancies; secondly, it might prove difficult to secure low handicap players – they would have to wait in the queue behind the wives, who might fill up the club to its agreed limit. In 1964, therefore, the Ladies' Captain had an interview with the Secretary, Mr Allen. The outcome was a happy one for the ladies because it was agreed that "the ladies should do exactly as they think fit in choosing those who can be elected to the Club". The next year the ladies adopted the policy of taking candidates "in order of application".

On the Course

Since a larger membership meant greater use of the course there were occasions when the ladies had to take action on their own behalf. In the 1950s there were several requests – eventually successful – to have the LGU tees correctly marked and properly tended.

There were discussions too about tee reservations and priority in 1963. The 1st tee was reserved for ladies' competitions between 1–2 p.m. on Thursdays and the 12th tee was also used as a second starting place. Although the ladies were unwilling to surrender their allotted priority on the 12th, they had to do so, and agree to alternate with other players. But in 1967 an extra half hour priority time was allowed for competitions so that the ladies had the 1st tee from 12.30 – 2 p.m. In 1972 the time allowed was extended from 11 a.m. to 2 p.m.

Mrs M Anstey in 1954. Devon County Ladies Champion 1950, 1952, 1953, 1954, 1960, 1965 and 1966. Mrs Anstey was a member at both East Devon and Exeter Golf Clubs for many years.

A request that was made in the early days – to have the greens cut for competition days – was repeated in the 1960s. To it was added a new one: that the greens should not be watered during ladies' competitions. The reply came back that "arrangements will be made whenever possible to obviate any inconvenience" and there the matter rested.

Competitions&Matches

A popular competition, the White Elephant, was begun in 1961. In 1963 it was brought forward to be played in March, "open to all members with or without a handicap". The "white elephants" brought along had to be worth about five shillings. In 1967 it was decided that competitors should be drawn "high handicap with low". The competition is now taken to mark the beginning of the spring season.

Entries for club competitions were running at about thirty in the 1960s and the Opens too were well supported. Entries for the 1964 and 1965 Opens had to be closed when the numbers reached eighty-eight. Prize money had been raised to £2 to the winner, £1 to the runner-up, usually given in vouchers for the Professional's shop.

Up until 1966, when the new practice ground beside the 1st hole was completed, members were allowed "to take practice shots before competitions on the side of the 18th hole", though it was forbidden "to play a putt on the green". After their rounds thirsty competitors went looking for tea which was not always available at this time because it was not served until 4 p.m. A request was made to bring the time forward to 3.30 p.m. on competition days "as so many ladies start playing from 12.00 pm and are back in the clubhouse from 3.00 pm onwards; they go home rather than wait nearly one hour for tea".

In the County the ladies continued their successes of the 1920s and 1930s by winning the coveted trophy, the Still Cup, in 1968, 1969 and 1972.

In 1966 the ladies widened their competition horizons further by requesting "they be allowed 8 home matches" so that they could enter for the Sheelah Creasy Bowl. Their request was granted by the men's committee and in the following year they went on to capture this newly started team event.

Standard Scratch Score

In 1948 the LGU fixed the SS of the course at 75. From January 1954 it came down again – to 73 – against the wishes of the Ladies' Committee. There it remained until March 1963, when a further cut of one was made. This new SS of 72 meant that the 9th was reduced from par 5 to par 4.

1975 – 2002

Membership Increases

The last twenty-five or so years have seen the ladies' section continue to flourish and to increase in numbers. In 1982 there were 99 members with current handicaps, in 2001 there were 160. (The ladies' allocation is approximately one third of the total club membership.) Attendance at Annual General Meetings rose from about 75 in the 1980s to over 90 as the century drew to a close.

The weighting of the membership in favour of the Bronze Division caused some concern at various times so that eventually a handicap limit was set for candidates on the waiting list. Initially 29, when the new handicap system was introduced in 1998, it was raised to 32.

In 1983 the scheme through which a number of ladies – called the Yearly Green Ticket holders – could take up annual temporary memberships was phased out and the following year the category Country Membership was also abolished.

Tee reservation time on Tuesday continued to be lengthened throughout this period, a development which was very necessary in view of the number wishing to play. Today it is usual for between 80 and 110 ladies to tee off on Tuesdays. Big occasions, like the Spring Meeting, always attract over one hundred.

Success in Competitions

The fixture list continued to be a full one with East Devon Ladies looking outside the domestic scene and playing their part – often very successfully – in county meetings and national competitions. Some changes were made in how the play was organised.

Still Cup Team 1969. Mrs Law, Mrs Pritchard, Mrs Pursey, Mrs Powell, Mrs Nankivell, Mrs Anstey, Mrs Curle, Mrs Orange and Mrs Hellyer-Jones.

In the mid-seventies, for example, it was decided to run competitions in support of local charities only, which were drawn from members' suggestions. This developed into the practice of the Lady Captain choosing her own special charity, for which funds were raised during her year of office. In this way many worthy causes have benefited.

1980 saw another alteration in the organisation of competitions. It was the first year when two Open Meetings were held, one for the Silver Division and one for the Bronze. Over and above this, for the last six or so years, a third Open has been held, a four-ball team event for handicaps from both divisions.

Invitation Day was restored to the calendar in 1983. It had been surrendered at a time when it was felt that ladies' events should not be too numerous, but it had always been popular because of the pleasure of returning the hospitality received on other courses.

The ladies continued to play in the two main Devon County team competitions, the Still Cup and the Sheelah Creasy Bowl. They had considerable success in both. The Still Cup team had "a purple patch" with successes in 1991, 1992 and 1993. 1992 was a particularly outstanding year because the Sheelah Creasy Bowl was also brought back to East Devon. There had been other successes in this competition in 1979, 1987 and 1989.

Sources of Revenue

The method of finding the finance to run competitions was changed in 1987 with the abolition of the Prize Fund. In this system members had voluntarily contributed a sum – usually about one pound – to help defray the cost of prizes and other expenses. The raising of the fees for entering monthly competitions was found to be a simple and adequate replacement.

There were, however, other sources of revenue. Bridge evenings, for example, organised by the members themselves, and begun in 1985, raised substantial sums for the ladies' club over the years.

Latterly, the Christmas Bazaars have performed the same function. The funds raised are used, not only for the Captain's charity, but for team expenses throughout the year. Depending on the draw, the Still Cup and Sheelagh Creasy teams can cover a good mileage during the season and the ladies' club has always paid for the petrol and match meals of its competitors.

There have also been individual acts of generosity. Members have allowed their homes and gardens to be used for bring-and-buy sales. Mrs Peggy Anstey, who was one such member, contributed a considerable sum for the ladies to spend as they thought fit. Part of the money was used to replace the Captain's brooch. The first one – called "a badge" – was bought in 1978 and was in the form of an enamel bar. In 1990 a silver pheasant brooch was chosen, which, until 1999, was presented at the AGM to the incoming Captain by her predecessor. When, however, it was decided that the men's Captain and the Lady Captain should both begin their terms of office on 1 January, the ceremonial hand-over of the brooch was switched to that date and took place after the drive-ins. This happened for the first time in 2001.

A Famous Name

1984 was the year that brought a famous golfer to East Devon. This was Mrs Marley Harris, or Marley Spearman as she was better known, England Champion in 1964, among many other successes, who had come to live in Budleigh Salterton. She was immediately offered full membership. Although she never took part in competitions, wishing, perhaps, for her play to be remembered when she as at the top of her game, she later played on the course when teaching her grandson the game.

Ladies' card 1990.

EAST DEVON LADIES' GOLF CLUB

NAME .... HANDICAP ....

COMPETITION .... DATE .... ALLOWANCE ....

Marker's Score	Hole	Yards	Par	Stroke Index	Player's Score	Win + Loss − Half 0 Points	Marker's Score	Hole	Yards	Par	Stroke Index	Player's Score	Win + Loss − Half 0 Points
	1	298	4	*15*				10	149	3	*16*		
	2	293	4	*13*				11	288	4	*10*		
	3	403	5	*3*				12	428	5	*2*		
	4	132	3	*17*				13	122	3	*18*		
	5	322	4	*7*				14	389	4	*4*		
	6	464	5	*11*				15	290	4	*12*		
	7	353	4	*1*				16	361	4	*8*		
	8	193	3	*9*				17	405	5	*6*		
	9	434	4	*5*				18	316	4	*14*		
	Out	2892	36					In	2748	36			
MARKER'S SIGNATURE								Out	2892	36			
								Total	5640	72			
PLAYER'S SIGNATURE							L.G.U.S.S. 72			Handicap			
							PAR 72			NET SCORE			

Amalgamation with the Men's Club

The ladies have always been willing to play their part in club life. In the seventies, when social events were starting to be more frequently organised, the "General Committee" came to rely on the ladies for certain aspects of these events, such as the arrangement of the flowers and the provision of catering. To spread the workload, it was agreed in 1977 that the Lady Captain could invite six lady members to serve under her as a Social Events Sub-committee, responsible for any necessary preparations. This system continued until 1984, when it was felt to have outlived its usefulness because the main club had set up its own Entertainments Committee, which the Lady Captain and Vice-Captain attended.

It seems that 1985 was the first year when amalgamation with the men's club was discussed by the Ladies' Committee – which voted "unanimously" against it, at least, "at the present time". Instead it requested that a lady member be allowed to attend main committee meetings, albeit in an unofficial capacity and without voting rights. The request was turned down as the men felt that their existing committee of fourteen members was quite large enough.

In 1988 it was noted that there would soon be legislation strengthening the Sex Discrimination Laws and that this "could have implications in Golf Clubs where there are different scales of subscription and consequently of facilities. The matter of voting rights also is a thorny question, likely to be the subject of comment."

No further move was made in the direction of amalgamation until May 1991, when the ladies wrote to the main committee asking for consideration to be given to ladies becoming "full voting members of East Devon Golf Club". A meeting with the men was then arranged in July, when the committee's request received sympathetic attention. It was decided that, on receipt of a suitably worded resolution from East Devon Ladies' Golf Club, an Extraordinary General Meeting of East Devon Golf Club would be called to vote on the ladies' request. Solicitors were asked to advise both clubs on the constitutional changes involved. In October the men's committee voted in favour of the ladies becoming full members. Its decision was ratified at the EGM on 5th December 1991.

New Handicap System

The latest change to affect all lady members was the introduction of the new handicapping system in 1998, described by the LGU as "sailing into uncharted waters" and by others as "baffling and bewildering"!

To many it was complicated and it certainly caused a great deal of work to those involved in implementing it.

However, after some experience of the new method, there seems to have been an acknowledgement that it is fairer and provides a truer record of a golfer's current play than earlier systems. This was revealed at the end of the 1999 season when 59 per cent of lady members either retained their handicap or reduced it.

A Century of Ladies Golf

As the century of ladies' golf at East Devon draws to a close, it is clear that today's members share many of the attributes of those who started out in 1902.

They want to play competitive golf. On every Tuesday throughout the year some sort of competition is organised for the ladies. This is in contrast to the approach of the men, who compete on two Saturdays a month.

The ladies are outward-looking, always keen to play on other courses, whether in friendly matches, mixed competitions or more serious play.

They are contributors. There have always been members willing to give of their time and expertise so that things will run smoothly, not only in their own section but in the club as a whole.

They are social, ready to provide and to enjoy that accompaniment to golf which is always there even after a disappointing round – namely, friendship. Even on a winter Tuesday, the course closed or play abandoned, many ladies of East Devon gather to have lunch together. Diaries are taken out, news exchanged and there is the buzz of sociability.

With such a solid tradition of good management and successful play behind it, it is understandable that this active section of a distinguished club can look forward to its next one hundred years with a happy confidence.

CHAPTER 12

An Exceptionally Scenic Course

SINCE THE DAY it was opened for play, the course has drawn plaudits for the beauty and variety of its scenery. Phrases such as "one of the most delightful places on the South Devon coast", "magnificent views unobtainable from any other course in the kingdom", "huge hills sloping away to high cliffs" are enough to suggest the appreciation by golfers down the years of the stunning panoramas afforded from many holes. In 1986 Peter Alliss wrote in his book The Good Golf Guide: "The club claims to have the finest variety of land and seascape in England. Few would argue with them."

Flora

At ground level too there is much to admire. John Orange, with his extensive knowledge of plants, has written authoritatively on what we can look out for on the course, and the following is drawn from his writing in 1999.

"The most striking of the ankle-high plants are the Orchids. We have three species, two quite common and one rare. The Green-winged Orchid has increased beyond expectations and can be found on eight holes. It flowers from mid-April to early May. The Heath Spotted Orchid, found in the rough between the 1st and 2nd fairways, flowers a little later. Our third orchid, the autumn-flowering Spiranthes (English name: Autumn Ladies Tresses) is most uncommon. Only three plants grow on the back of a bunker on the 5th.

"Many of us have watched with pleasure the spread of the Harebell colonies on the left of the 16th hole. Here too are mats of thyme. In conjunction with the yellow Birds-foot Trefoil it makes a memorable sight.

"On the right of the 8th tee some players may have noticed, while waiting for the green to clear, large globular seed-heads like those of the dandelion but twice as large. These belong to the Goatsbeard or Jack-go-to-bed-at-noon, whose flowers open only in the morning. It is generally common but appears nowhere else on the course.

"The Common Dodder, which is parasitic on gorse and heather, can be found almost anywhere on the course. It appears as an odd network of reddish threads. It has tiny, bell-shaped flowers and a pungent scent which, once experienced, will not easily be forgotten.

"These are the most striking of our low-growing plants but there are others no less interesting for not being showy. They include the following:

Common Milkwort, flowering in early May, chiefly on the 11th.

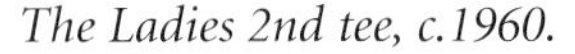

The Ladies 2nd tee, c.1960.

Lousewort, a most attractive plant despite its name, which derives from its being a supposed remedy for head lice. Its bright pink flowers, opening from April onwards, can be seen around the ditch and in the rough short of the green on the 13th.

Eyebright, widespread in the short rough.

Ground Ivy, is not an ivy but a member of the Thyme family. It is a pungent plant with blue flowers and is widespread.

"Perhaps the rarest of our low-growing plants is one most likely to be passed over, and that is the Pale Heath Violet, which is very much like the Heath Dog Violet except that its flowers are usually pale milky blue and may be almost white. We have found no more than half a dozen over the years.

"Heathers are the plants we use least kindly on the course. Like the grass itself they are taken for granted. They can be, and are, trodden down, flattened by heavy trolleys, cut up by golf clubs and generally misused without thought. There is a limit to the amount of punishment they can stand, however, and we are near to the limit in some places.

"We have two types of common heather, the Bell Heather, the earlier of the two to flower, and the Ling. They will put up with all the unnatural interference that is necessary in course maintenance. They have no enemy, at least not in these parts, but ourselves.

"We have large numbers of taller plants, of course, that survive where they are not mown, including Rosebay and wild raspberries."

Harry Stocker was another member of the club who not only enjoyed our lovely course but wrote about it with real knowledge. Here he is talking about fungi in 1980:

"Many varieties of fungi thrive when the wet conditions prevail. Most of them are edible, especially the large horse mushrooms that lots of players kick over. They have much more flavour than the field mushroom.

There is sometimes a crop of Parasol mushrooms near the 8th tee. This is a long-stemmed fungi with a rough skin. It looks like a partially opened parasol until ripe, when it opens to a flat top. It has white gills and is said to have a pleasant nutty flavour."

Fauna

Harry continues by describing the animals and birds of East Devon.

"Our fauna is mainly nocturnal and we rarely see the foxes or deer. Since the clearing of the clover below the 8th the deer seem to have stopped summering between the 12th and 17th holes. If you care to stroll at daybreak I am sure you will be rewarded with a view of these lovely creatures around the 7th and 8th.

"Rabbits, stoats, weasels and voles are plentiful. I have had at least four good meals by robbing a stoat of its prey. I still find adders hacked to pieces by nervous people. They are very shy creatures and disappear at the first approach. I found a handsome specimen on the 12th one year and visited him every sunny round for three months.

"The widening of the fairways and the lessening of the rough over the years has largely contributed to the decline of the lark population. A few years ago there were hundreds. From January to October one was never out of earshot of a lark if the sun was shining. I have found dozens of nests on the course. Now there are about three pairs and they are nesting off the course.

"The lovely Yellowhammer always demands attention as he sits on top of a gorse bush repeating his tuneful ditty – "Little bit of bread and no cheese". There are still plenty of Linnets, Finches and Warblers. I have seen a flock of 27 Long-tailed tits on the 6th and often see Goldcrests and Nuthatches in the firs behind that green.

"On a summer evening the Nightjar can be heard and seen at dusk in the deep rough on the right of the 7th hole. We Devonians call it the "fern owl". It has a beautiful gliding flight and is a competent ventriloquist with an unmistakable whirring, vibrating call."

John Orange now takes up the story. Writing in 1981, he said:

"My favourite bird, one that we are fortunate to have on the course all the year round, is the Raven. It nests on the nearby cliffs from February onwards and makes its presence known by its deep honking call, quite different from that of any comparable bird. It is one of the very few birds that will on occasion fly upside down, apparently from joie de vivre, if that concept has any significance in the avian world. Two ravens will make a buzzard's life unbearable, by harrying, swooping and pecking. Such encounters are often to be seen, especially over the seaward holes.

"Buzzards often appear over the course, though as far as I know, none nests in the area. Buzzards sometimes take some of the multitude of rabbits that we have, particularly on the higher holes. Swallows continue to nest in one or two of the shelter huts. What all this amounts to is a treasure trove of nature, a wealth of beauty and interest to be not only enjoyed but preserved by us all."

Over the last few years the number of Peregrine falcons seen above the course has greatly increased. The buzzards are back after an absence, despite occasional harrying by crows and gulls.

Trees

Once again John Orange was to the fore in adding to the natural beauties of the course he knows so well. He explains some of the salient features.

"A great many trees have been planted in the last half century or so, including the line of mixed species separating the 5th from the 9th. (*See picture on page 28.*) These were planted by Colonel Honeyman, a former secretary. Incidentally, he was respected, sometimes feared, for suffering neither slow play nor the slightest lapse from proper behaviour on the course.

"I wrote in 1981 that the stand of Scots Pines on the right of the 13th hole was beginning to deteriorate. Whether or not this was caused by the onset of the honey-fungus that eventually killed about half of them I do not know; but some remain, and I hope they will go on.

"I and some others, appointed by different committees, had a hand in planting some conifers designed to influence the play of a few holes, notably the 15th and 16th. There was a time when a loose fluffed drive to the right of the 15th, provided the ball did not reach the bunker, could open the way to an easy shot to the green. The committee decided to have a stand of trees beyond the bunker, and George Peaker and I planted them.

"While we were working, a member who was playing the hole came over and said: 'Whatever are you planting those for? They don't plant trees at St. Andrews, and that ought to be good enough for us.' He was quite serious. Neither of us could think of an adequate reply. Two days later we found that each of the little trees had been pulled out of its hole, broken across the middle, and placed neatly by the hole. We left the replanting for a month. This time the trees survived.

"I will mention a couple of other plantings only. The first is that on the right of the 7th hole, where more than 50 decorative trees were planted, which are very attractive now and will be outstandingly so in the future. This planting was instigated and supervised by the late Phipps Turnbull. Perhaps I may be forgiven for saying that the quite large horse chestnut which stands on the right of the 7th, near the elm, was given to the club by my wife and myself, to fill in near the elm which had to be cut down because of the universal disease. We got the tree, which was supposed to be a slightly unusual hybrid, more interesting than the common horse chestnut, from a specialist firm. But it turned out to be quite ordinary.

"The late N.D.G. ('Jimmy') James, Clinton Devon Land Agent and a noted authority on trees, collected in 1991 acorns from several famous oaks, including the Crimea Oak at Althorp, and grew seedlings from them. These eventually found their way into my wife's care, and she grew them on for some years before giving them to the golf club, to be planted at the lower end of the 9th hole, on the left. The birch trees near them were put there to make a shelter, the intention being that they should be removed in due course. A few of the oaks died or were damaged and replacements from the same source were put in. No reserve remains, however.

"These oaks will never reach the stature of the originals, of course, there being not nearly enough depth of soil. There is nearby as fine a specimen of an oak as is likely to be found in this environment, the one on the left near the start of the 5th hole; perhaps some of Jimmy James' oaks may grow as well. One more tree is worth a mention, and that is the aspen on the right of the 7th green, the only aspen on the course. It used to be distinctively V-shaped, and I wrote in 1981 that it seems sometimes to mock one's best efforts to reach the green. But now it seems more in one piece, and incidentally is much larger."

Golf and Golfers on West Down

MANY AND VARIED have been the visitors to the club over the years, but from time to time nationally known figures have played on the course and it is these occasions which are remembered in this chapter.

Braid, Taylor, Vardon and Herd

The club approached James Braid, the winner of the Open, in 1903, not to come and play an exhibition match but to advise on course reconstruction. Braid was a prolific golf course architect with, eventually, over one hundred original courses to his name and over fifty conversions of nine-hole courses to ones of eighteen holes. Chamier thought his terms "very reasonable" but nothing came of the initiative.

In 1905 there was talk locally of Vardon and Taylor coming to Sidmouth in November. Some members at East Devon wished to get up a subscription for the professionals to play here also, but the Secretary, Whytock, felt that November

The Golf Champions at Salterton.

Exmouth Journal. 1. Aug 1908

GOLF AT SALTERTON.

CHAMPIONS AT PLAY.

BRAID, TAYLOR, VARDON AND HERD.

Summer weather prevailed at Budleigh Salterton on Thursday, for the opening of the two days' professional golf tournament on the links of the East Devon Club. James Braid (open champion), J. H. Taylor (French champion), Harry Vardon, and Alex Herd were the players, each of the last three being ex-champions. The four have won twelve championships between them. Taylor is a native of North Devon, and learnt his golf on the Westward Ho! links, which, after matches at Sidmouth, the players are to visit. Large numbers of people attended from all parts of the county, and followed the game with keen interest over the beautiful links. Lord Clinton, the president of the Club, generously gave £100 for prize money, and Mr. W. Whytock, the hon. secretary, was concerned with the arrangements. Luncheon and tea marquees were erected near the pavilion.

Braid, Taylor, and Vardon are a remarkable trio of sportsmen, all about the same age. These three, for the past few years, have had a monopoly of the open championship such as, it is probable, no three will ever have again. Taylor was the first to gain prominence by securing the championship in 1894 and 1895. In 1896, Vardon and Taylor tied for first place, Vardon winning on the play off; in 1902 there was a tie between Vardon and Braid for second place, and in 1904 there was a tie between Taylor and Braid for second place. Three times has the triumvirate occupied the top three places in the premier event, but the monopoly was destroyed last year, when Massy (who is a Frenchman) wrested it from the Englishmen. Some disappointment was felt at Massy's inability to be present.

The record for the Salterton course is 71, held by Mr. C. C. Aylmer (Sidmouth).

The senior stewards were Colonel H O Walker, Mr E Chamier, Mr John Oliver, and Captain Cooke. The scorers, Messrs C C Aylmer, F Cobbett, C E Pine-Coffin, and W Whytock. The stewards of the course of the first match were Major Evans, Major Wadmore, Captain Edwards, Messrs S R Baker, R W Friend, F J C Hunter, R Chichester, M B Ford. Second course, Col Burgman, Messrs A P Percival, W Ferrier Kerr, H Herford, H S Ellis, P de Putron, S G Budd, and G B Young.

Thursday's play consisted of a 36-hole stroke competition, for prizes of £20, £12, £8, and £5, and £5 for the best score of 18 holes. Braid and Taylor were the first to start at 11 o'clock, and a quarter of an hour later, Herd and Vardon commenced. A. Massy was to have taken part, but he telegraphed from Versailles to say that indisposition would prevent his attendance, and Herd, who has just recently created a record at the Huddersfield link, accordingly took his place. Braid, Taylor, and Vardon arrived on Wednesday, and played a match arranged with members of the Club during the afternoon. The greens were in excellent order for the champions.

Appended are the details of the play:

FIRST ROUND.

Taylor:
Out .... 4 4 4 5 4 6 5 4 4—40
Home ...... 4 5 4 3 3 4 4 3 4—34
Total 74

Braid:
Out .... 3 5 5 3 4 5 4 4 4—37
Home ...... 3 6 4 3 4 4 6 4 4—38
Total 75

Herd:
Out .... 4 4 4 4 4 6 5 5 5—41
Home ...... 3 5 4 4 5 4 4 4 4—47
Total 78

Vardon:
Out .... 4 4 3 5 4 5 5 5 5—40
Home ...... 3 5 5 4 3 5 8 3 4—40
Total 80

SECOND ROUND.

Taylor:
Out .... 3 4 4 4 4 6 5 5 4—39
Home ...... 4 5 4 4 4 4 7 3 5—40
Total 79

Braid:
Out .... 4 3 4 5 4 5 5 3 5—38
Home ...... 2 5 4 6 4 3 6 3 4—37
Total 75

Vardon:
Out .... 2 4 3 4 5 5 4 5 5—37
Home ...... 4 6 4 4 5 4 6 3 5—41
Total 78

Herd:
Out .... 3 4 5 4 4 6 6 5 4—41
Home ...... 3 5 4 4 4 4 5 4 4—37
Total 78

Totals:—
Braid 150
Taylor 153
Herd 156
Vardon 158

Braid did not start particularly well in the morning. He was short with the down-hill putt at the second hole, and missed a rather short one at the third. At the fourth he holed out from a distance of nearly 20 yards, and after that played very well, except at the eleventh, where he took three putts, and at the sixteenth, when he was in a ditch. In the afternoon he broke his cleek at the fourth hole in playing out of a deep cup and at the thirteenth he was unlucky, being on the edge of the green with a brassie shot from the tee, but the ball being almost unplayable in the rough ground, he took six. Especially taking into consideration his experience of several pieces of ill-luck, the champion played a sound game. Taylor showed best form in the homeward half of the first round, when his approaching and putting were very fine. At the sixteenth, during the afternoon, he had a seven, his tee shot being badly in the rough. Herd was off the line several times before lunch, but played some clever approaches after.

Vardon was very unfortunate at the 16th hole, where his ball got into an unplayable spot among the gorse, and had to be picked out, by which he lost two strokes. He started very well in the second round, and holed a long putt for two at the first. In fact, going out, he played almost perfect golf, but got into difficulties several times coming home.

The general standard of the play was very good, considering the tricky character of the course, on account of the number of slopes, especially for approaching. The greens particularly, and the course too, were in need of rain, but some of the strokes were beautifully judged, and an appreciation of the play was frequently extended to the professionals.

YESTERDAY'S PLAY.

Yesterday's play consisted of a 36 holes match play four ball foursome—Braid and Herd versus Taylor and Vardon—for £15 each first prize, and £10 each for the second. The weather continued perfect, and there was again a large attendance. The scores were:—

FIRST ROUND.

Braid and Herd:
Out .... 3 4 4 4 4 5 4 4 4—36
Home ...... 3 5 4 3 4 3 4 3 4—33
Total 69

Taylor and Vardon:
Out .... 4 3 4 3 4 5 4 5 4—36
Home ...... 3 5 4 4 4 4 5 3 4—36
Total 72

SECOND ROUND.

Braid and Herd:
Out .... 3 4 3 4 5 4 3 5 4—35
Home ...... 2 5 3 3 4 3 4 3 3—30
Total 65

Taylor and Vardon:
Out .... 4 5 4 4 4 4 4 4 4—37
Home ...... 3 6 4 4 3 4 5 3 3—35
Total 72

Braid and Herd won, eight up and six to play.

Mr E Chamier apologised for the absence of Lord Clinton, who was detained in London by Parliamentary duties, and called upon Mr F Cobbett, the Club Captain, to present the prizes. Braid thanked the club for the hospitable way the professionals had been treated, and for the generous prizes, and cheers for Lord Clinton and the Hon. Sec. concluded the proceedings.

Mr. T. F. Parker, of Salterton, catered, and Mr. R. M. Flint, of Exeter, supplied the tents.

CHAMPION GOLFERS IN DEVONSHIRE.

The golf champion and ex-champions were playing at Budleigh Salterton, yesterday and the day before. To-day they will be at Sidmouth, and next week at Westward Ho! Taylor and Herd are seated, the Devonshireman (Taylor) being on the left. The two who are standing are Braid, this year's champion, on the left, and Vardon on the right. Photograph by Mr. Blackburn, Salterton.

Golf Champions at East Devon in 1908 – Report of the Braid Match.

The Golf Champions at Salterton.

was too late in the year. "We had better wait till next season and then have some of the best professionals down when we open the new holes for play." This is a reference to two new holes laid out in the field which now contains the present 4th green, 5th fairway and the bottom of the 9th.

These holes were in play when Whytock wrote to Braid in February 1907, proposing a summer tournament. Braid replied that it would be better to have "a few of the best players by invitation in place of a larger field of poor ones", and this was accepted.

Probably because, as Whytock remarked, "the best professionals make their engagements so long beforehand", it was not until August 1908 that the match took place, over two days. It was covered extensively by the Exmouth Journal.

Australian Connection: Donald Bradman

In December 1934 the famous Australian batsman Don Bradman arrived in Budleigh for a short holiday while convalescing from an operation for appendicitis. He stayed with a member of the club, Mr H. O. Sykes, who, before retiring, had been managing director of a sports goods manufacturer in Yorkshire. He had got to know Bradman six years earlier and explained the circumstances in an interview with the Journal.

"I was present at the third Test Match at Melbourne in January 1929, when Don Bradman first came to the fore and created a sensation by scoring 79 in the first innings and 112 in the second. I realised at once that here was a great new batsman and I got into touch with him and secured a ten years' contract with him to autograph our cricket bats. He has come down as the result of a long-standing invitation and is just lolling about and enjoying himself quietly. Mr Bradman likes the district very much. He has played a little bridge and has been up to the Golf Club that has kindly extended its amenities to him, if he cares to use them. Mr. Bradman, however, is not yet able to play golf, but he has enjoyed the social side of the club life.

"He went to the entertainment at the Public Hall last night and thoroughly enjoyed the programme. He also went out to the meet of the Otter Vale Beagles at Weston, Salcombe Regis. He is sailing for Australia on the Orient Line steamship "Otranto" and will spend Christmas at sea. He hopes to be fit enough to take up cricket again in the next Australian season and it is his belief that his illness will not affect his career in any way."

Henry Cotton's Visit

In April 1944 Mr Livesey, as acting Secretary, wrote to the estate with an appeal. "Please do your utmost about petrol. [There was strict rationing.] The famous Henry Cotton is playing an Exhibition Match here on Sunday."

Cotton had won the Open twice. In the match he partnered Captain F. H. Waters (Royal and Ancient, Handicap 1) against Arnold Stickley, R.A.F. (East Devon and the son of the club's recently deceased Professional) and Lieutenant Colonel Cutler (Deal, scratch). The proceeds went to the Red Cross and the St John Prisoner-of-War Fund, for which Cotton had already raised £50,000.

Championship Meeting

In July 1946 the West of England section of the Professional Golfers' Association held a meeting at East Devon over two days, when the West of England Championship was played for, followed by the qualifying rounds for the News of the World Tournament.

The draw included: Max Faulkner, R. A. Whitcombe, C. Ward, P. Alliss and T. Haliburton. Among West Country professionals taking part were: L. W. Dymond (Teignmouth), Gus Faulkner (West Bay), R. J. James (Stover), G. Easterbrook (Sidmouth), H. E. Osborne (Newquay), J. A. Learmouth and J. D. Learmouth (Lelant) and O. J. Stickley and A. J. Robins (East Devon).

Championship Day

The Exmouth Journal reported that there were "no thrills" but "plenty of good, steady play". The course was "in first class condition" and the greens "perfect" though "on the slow side" for the time of year. In general, the players were criticised for their putting, "consistently declining to give the hole a chance".

Reg Whitcombe (Parkstone) led the field with a 71 in the morning but in the afternoon lost his chance of winning on the 8th. His drive reached the edge of the green but he then three putted. Tom Haliburton (Knowle), playing later, reached the 15th "in three under fours". A five on the 16th "cut things fine" but he followed this with two fours.

The leading results were:

T. Haliburton	142
R. A. Whitcombe	143
P. Alliss	145
A. J. Robins	147

It is interesting to note that among the players was A. D. Mercer, listed as "unattached". He was to be Secretary at East Devon from 1971 to 1980.

The bogey for the 6293 yards course was 73.

The News of the World Qualifying Rounds

The four qualifiers were:

R. A. Whitcombe (Parkstone)	145
T. B. Haliburton (Knowle)	146
A. J. Robins (East Devon)	149
P. Alliss (Ferndown)	150

Guests for the day at East Devon were Sir John H. Amory, President of the Devon County Alliance of Professional and Amateur Golfers, and Lady Amory, who, before her marriage, was Joyce Wethered.

Ryder Cup Stars

The Exhibition Match featuring four Ryder Cup players – Peter Alliss, Bernard Hunt, Dai Rees and Dave Thomas – that was held at East Devon in August 1966 was a great success. Not only did some 450 spectators have the chance to see "some really superb shots" but also they helped to raise over £150, after expenses, for the Forces Help Society and Lord Roberts' Workshops.

Alliss and Hunt started well when the former birdied the 1st but thereafter they struggled to contain the Welshmen and eventually lost two

Month	Day	Fixture
April	1	County Medal
,,	5	Medal: Heslop Cup Finals
,,	8	Bogey
,,	13	Lyme Regis "B" (Away)
,,	14	Still Cup Team v. EDGC
,,	17	Spring Meeting and Extra Medal (p.m. only)
,,	18	Spring Meeting (p.m. only)
,,	19	Bogey: Coronation Cup Finals
,,	20	Palairet Trophy: 1st Round at Exeter
,,	22	Medal
,,	25	Sheelah Creasy Bowl v. Axe Cliff (Home)
,,	26	The Silver Putter
,,	27	Two Club Competition
,,	27	Two Club Competition
May	2	Prudential Assurance Co. 25 (p.m. only)
,,	3	Medal and Rolle Cup
,,	6	County Medal
,,	7	News Trade Assoc. 40 (p.m. only)
,,	10	Club Pheasant
,,	11	Sidmouth "B" (Home)
,,	13	Bogey
,,	14	Veterans Cup
,,	16	Match v. Devon Constabulary (Evening)
,,	18	Devon Open Championship
,,	20	Coronation Foursomes
,,	24	Guide Dogs Competition
,,	25	Guide Dogs Competition
,,	26	Guide Dogs Competition
,,	27	Medal
,,	28	Still Cup v. Exeter (Home 1.15 p.m.)
,,	30	Exeter "A" (Away)
,,	31	Bogey and Pine Coffin Cup
June	1	Target Golf Competition
,,	1	Target Golf Competition
,,	1	Aplin Foursomes (Start of)
,,	2	Still Cup v. Yelverton (Home 1.15 p.m.)
,,	3	County Medal
June	6	Sheelah Creasy Bowl v. Honiton (Home)
,,	7	Medal and Warn Cup
,,	8	Sidmouth Picture Match (Away)
,,	10	Bogey
,,	12	Sheelah Creasy Bowl v. Exeter (Home)
,,	14	Captain's Team v. Seniors
,,	15	Teignmouth "A" and "B" (Away)
,,	17	Medal
,,	21	Bogey and Cobbett Cup
,,	22	Lyme Regis "B" (Home)
,,	24	Open Meeting (a.m. and p.m.)
,,	28	Handicap Challenge Cup 1st Round
,,	29	Tiverton "A" and "B" (Home)
July	1	County Medal
,,	5	Medal and Handicap Challenge Cup 2nd Round
,,	6	Mystery Competition
,,	6	Mystery Competition
,,	8	Bogey and King George Fund for Sailors
,,	10	Seniors Cup
,,	13	Dawlish Warren "A" and "B" (Away)
,,	15	Extra Medal
,,	18	Match v. Devon Constabulary (Evening)
,,	19	Bogey
,,	22	Captains Prize and Medal
,,	27	Palairet Trophy Finals
,,	29	Playing Fields Foursomes
Aug.	1	Sheelah Creasy Bowl v. Sidmouth (Home)
,,	2	Medal
,,	3	Sidmouth "B" (Away)
,,	5	County Medal
,,	6	Daily Telegraph Boys and Girls Competition
,,	8	Exeter "A" (Home: Evening)
,,	12	Bogey and All England Competition
,,	13	Mixed Foursomes Cup
,,	15	Warn Junior Cup
,,	16	Bogey
Aug.	17	Tiverton "A" and "B" (Away)
,,	19	Extra Medal
,,	23	Captain's Prize
,,	26	Medal
,,	27	Ladies v. Men
Sept.	2	County Medal
,,	6	Medal and Scratch Medal
,,	9	Bogey
,,	13	Club Pheasant
,,	14	Sidmouth Picture Match (Home)
,,	14	Wood Trophy (Start of)
,,	15	Autumn Meeting and Extra Medal (p.m. only)
,,	16	Autumn Meeting (p.m. only)
,,	19	British Dental Assoc.
,,	20	Bogey
,,	21	Dawlish Warren "A" and "B" (Home)
,,	22	English Ladies Golf Assoc. (S.W. Div.) (Course Closed)
,,	23	English Ladies Golf Assoc. (S.W. Div.)
,,	24	English Ladies Golf Assoc. (S.W. Div.)
,,	25	English Ladies Golf Assoc. (S.W. Div.) Finals
,,	27	Open Meeting
,,	28	Open Meeting
,,	30	Medal
Oct.	4	Medal
,,	7	County Medal
,,	14	Bogey
,,	18	Bogey
,,	19	Match v. Town Club
,,	23	Captain v. Secretary's Teams
,,	28	Medal
Nov.	1	Medal
,,	4	County Medal
,,	8	Ladies A.G.M.
,,	11	Bogey

Fixtures card for 1969.

and one. Thomas, out in 33, had an excellent chance of beating the course record of 68, held jointly by Alliss and Norman Sutton (Exeter). However, on the 18th, needing only a birdie for the record, he drove across the gorse on the right and failed to reach the green. The exhibition was the thirteenth of nineteen matches the four played around the country in aid of their chosen charities.

Golf Fanatics International

GFI was an organisation of about 150 members who met at various courses round the country. The members subscribed for, and later presented, a powered wheelchair to a handicapped child. Nine of its members came from East Devon, which was described in its 1976 newsletter as "that super Club". Frank Twiselton held the post of President for one year.

GFI paid two visits to the club during Bobby Charlton's presidency. It came again in August 1975 when Val Doonican had taken over. He brought along Ronnie Corbett for the day. Entry fees for this tournament and others before it enabled a £300 electrically operated wheelchair to be presented to fourteen-year-old Wayne Chichester, disabled with a rare skin disease, who was being treated at Stoke Lyne Hospital. Both stars enjoy a game of golf and it was clearly a fun and rewarding day. A draw organised by Mr Iles, the club Steward, raised £100 towards a new gymnasium at the hospital.

In May 1977 Val Doonican led the Fanatics in a return visit to the club. This time the wheelchair was donated to Vranch House, Exeter for little Lisa Chinnery, aged nine. It was the 30th chair to be provided by the group in less than two and a half years.

Another Australian: Richie Benaud

In the same month as the Fanatics' visit, five Australian Test Cricketers were invited down to play on the course. 1977 was both the year of the club's 75th anniversary and of the Queen's Silver Jubilee. As part of the national celebrations a tree-planting programme was under way throughout the country. Accordingly, the five cricketers – Richie Benaud, Richie Robinson, Doug Walters, Greg Chappell and Ian Chappell – were asked to plant five eucalyptus trees behind the first tee. Only three large ones remain.

A year later, in September 1978, Richie

Benaud returned to the club at the invitation of the Captain, George Law, and unveiled a plinth in front of the trees as a permanent reminder of the planting session and of the golf the Australians had enjoyed on more than one occasion at East Devon.

In May 1977 Val Doonican led the Fanatics who included Ronnie Corbett, on a visit and presented a further wheelchair to Exeter's Vranch House.

BRIAN BARNES AND MAX FAULKNER

The celebrations were carried on in August when Brian Barnes and Max Faulkner (*see page 74*) played an exhibition match partnered by David Howard, the club's popular Professional, and Alan Richards, in front of a crowd of about 300. It was reported that both "thought our greens were quite good" and had "enjoyed the course".

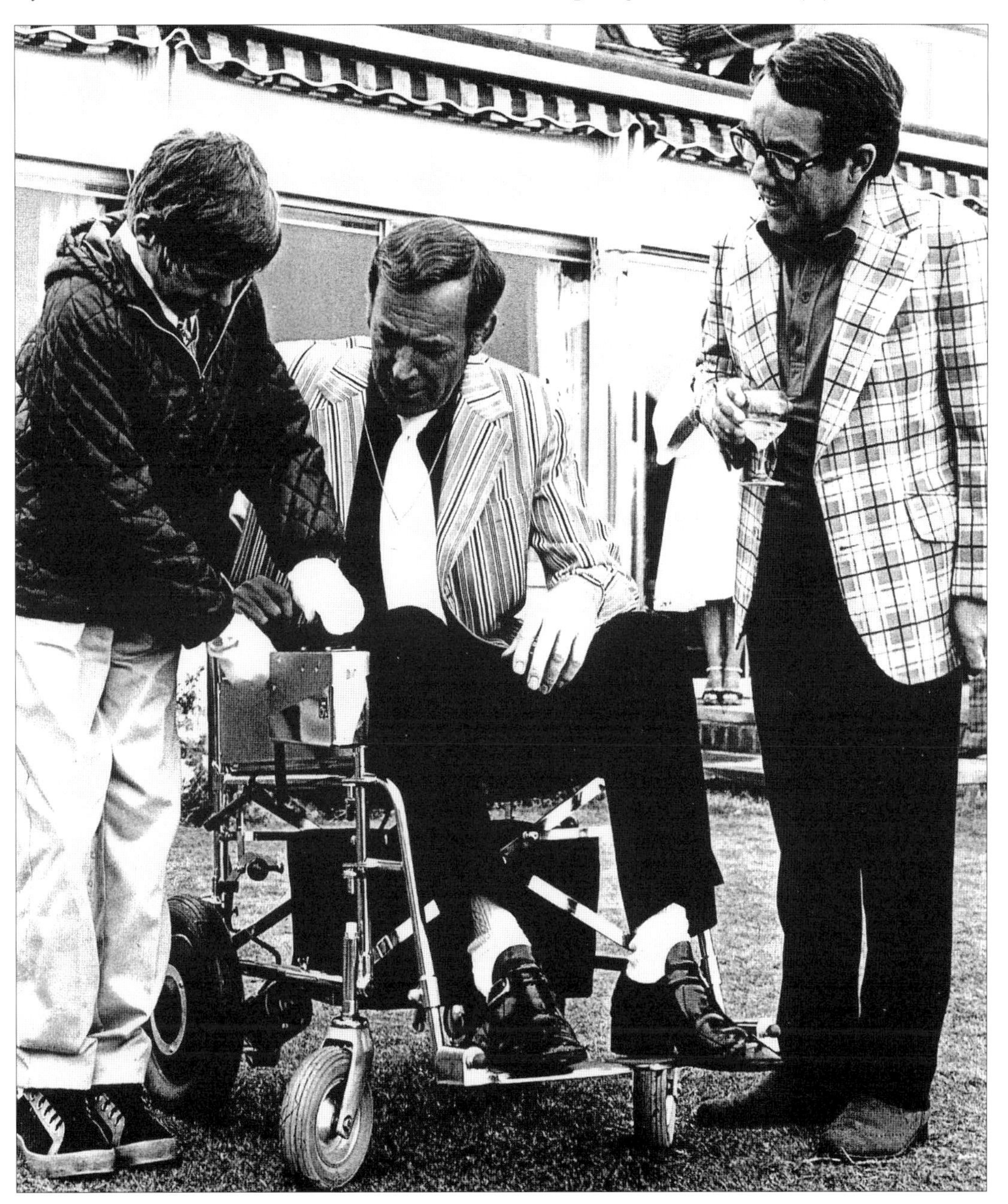

CHAPTER 14

1980 to the Present Day

There was some discussion in 1982 about the possibility of enhancing the club's facilities. The building of a 9-hole course – or even another 18-hole course – was mooted together with the provision of ancillary sports such as squash and tennis. The clubhouse could be extended and perhaps a swimming pool added. Although there was doubt about the financing of these wide-ranging ideas, Hamilton-Stutt was asked to advise on the potential for further golf. As it turned out, the proposals for these "momentous" improvements came to nothing. Had they been carried out, the character of the club would have been totally altered.

The nineties in particular were a busy time for the club, with development in all aspects of its life: the course, the clubhouse, the constitution and administrative structure. These changes, painstakingly thought through, enabled the club to keep abreast of modern trends and thus continue to offer the best possible golf, supported by a number of social activities held in a smart and welcoming clubhouse.

Course Management

A good deal of work was necessary over 1982 and 1983 to bring in the Standard Scratch Score and Handicapping Scheme as imported from Australia by the Council of National Golf Unions. As required, the course was remeasured by laser in October 1982 at a cost of £120. New tee markers had to be provided, though the temptation to save money by having markers "bearing advertising material" was resisted.

Irrigation System

The updating of the irrigation system was perhaps the most important task which had to be addressed. In 1992 leaks were discovered in the pipework leading to the 6th, 9th and 12th holes but the viability of the reservoir, and of the whole system itself, was suspect. These early fears were realised when firstly, in 1995, the supplementary pump, sited behind the 11th tee, had to be replaced at a cost of £1000, and secondly, and more seriously, when the tank developed a leak. As a result the course was without water during the summer months of 1996 until Watermation repaired the damage in the autumn. In the following year serious thought was given to the replacement of the whole system at an estimated cost of £50,000.

Running alongside the plan for repairing or replacing the irrigation system was the scheme to bring more water on to the course. The installation of a second storage tank would double capacity to 25,000 gallons and allow new areas, such as the tees, to be watered.

Another idea which was pursued from 1993 to 1995 was the sinking of a bore hole. Expert advice – including that of a water diviner – reported that it could probably be done on land behind the 5th tee at a likely cost of £15,000, but the project was abandoned in December 1995 because no water was found during drilling.

Advice was also sought on the feasibility of constructing "an environmental lake" for winter storage of water. Applications for funds – for the provision of the lake and a new irrigation system costed at £150,000 – were made to both the Royal and Ancient and the National Lottery, but unfortunately, neither was successful. Although planning permission was granted for the lake in 1998 by East Devon District Council the scheme had to be dropped in early 1999 when it was discovered that construction would have interfered with South West Water's pipelines.

In the end a consultant was called in to advise

on the reconditioning of the existing system. By the end of 1999 phases 1 and 2 had been completed at a cost of £70,000.

The First Tee

The sum of £10,000 was set aside in February 1999 for the refurbishment of the 1st tee. Work went ahead smoothly and was completed by the end of the year.

Repairing Fairways

During the 1990s there was, on occasion, quite serious concern over wear on the fairways, particularly the 1st and 2nd, which were sometimes used as an unofficial practice ground. In October 1992 winter rules were brought into effect early as a means of protection. A programme of top dressing the most distressed fairways, first undertaken in 1991, was also recommended. In 1995 this treatment had to be repeated. The following year a trial of vertidraining the fairways was undertaken.

At this time there was some discussion about the necessity of maintaining the link with the Sports Turf Research Institute at Bingley but, not surprisingly perhaps, it was decided that it was a valuable source of advice. It had, for example, been consulted in 1989 amid worries that the heather was beginning to die back. The advice was that this was because it was being trimmed too frequently in order to control the grass growing amongst it. The opposite procedure must be adopted. Both should be allowed to grow and eventually the heather would dominate. The gorse must be cut back almost to ground level. Various trials were carried out on selective grass killers to encourage growth and members were warned not to take their trolleys into the heather. Successive committees did what they could to raise awareness of the need to conserve the environment.

Inevitably the state of the fairways raised the question of the proper use of trolleys. Bans were enforced as required but there was always an awareness that this might prevent some members from playing.

The other question that the state of the fairways raised was the heavy volume of play over the course. There was no easy solution. The distinction of the club and the course ensured that there was always a waiting list for admission. Visitors brought in a valuable income but their impact on playing conditions had to be carefully monitored. A compromise was reached by making Thursdays a "society day" and leaving the rest of the week for members to enjoy their own course.

There was one factor, of course, which was always unpredictable: nature! In August 1995 lightning hit the 3rd fairway. The greens staff in the nearby sheds were shaken up and the strike left a sizeable pit in the ground. This, however, was successfully repaired, as was the breakdown in the electrics of the irrigation system also caused by the thunderbolt. (*See illustration of newspaper report on pages 112 and 113.*)

Attention to Bunkers...

The Hamilton Stutt programme for improving the bunkers continued in 1982 and 1983 on the bunkers of the 2nd, 4th, 5th, 8th, 13th and 15th holes. In the winter of 1985 drainage was incorporated into other bunkers using a treatment called Terran Layering. Still not satisfied that all was being done that could be done, the committee asked for a "a complete study of all 58 bunkers" to be made in January 1986.

Experiments were carried out "to find an ideal sand for each bunker on the course so that it will be possible to play out without undue difficulty under all weather conditions and so as to retain the sand in the bunkers when the wind blows".

Some years later, in 1993, a recommendation from the Greens Sub-Committee to open up the gap between the bunkers on the 11th fairway was approved and carried out. In the same year the faces of the front bunkers on the 4th were revetted and the grass bunker on the right of the 5th was demolished and a grass mound made in its place.

Twenty-five tons of Moneystone sand were bought for trial in the bunkers of the 10th, 11th and 18th in 1997. The success of the experiment meant that the remaining bunkers were replenished for an outlay of £5000.

In 1980 the marrying of the two bunkers on the east side of the 13th green was completed. At the same time the fairways bunkers on the 12th and 16th holes were grassed over.

The Journal, Thursday, July 27th., 1995

Lightning blasts golf course

●Thomas and Jonathan Holland view the damage during a morning round with their father.

ref. 982/21a

GOLFERS at East Devon Golf Club had a new bunker to avoid on Wednesday – after lightning carved a 15-foot trench along the third fairway.

Greenkeepers Wyndam Potter, Marcus Scott and Peter Newcombe sheltering in the machinery store thought they had been holed-in-one when the lightning struck during a storm at 7am.

The building shook, the lights went out and the three ducked for cover as they heard an enormous explosion.

By the time they got out of the building they were able to see a cloud of dust rising into the air from the fairway.

Mr Potter, Deputy Head Greenkeeper, said: "It was thundering and lightning when we got to work at about 5.45am so we sat in the shed. Then there was a terrific bang, the shed shook, and we thought we were goners.

"I've never seen anything like it in my life. It was terrifying.

"It was really eerie when we came out. Everything was very quiet and we could just see a big ball of dust coming out of the ground. It was so weird walking up to the green."

The giant crater was in the centre of the fairway, with scorch marks surrounding it, just feet away from trees lining the green.

John Tebbet, secretary of the club, said: "It is amazing that it didn't hit any of the trees or do any serious damage to anyone, it was a godsend really."

But dedicated golfers still continued to use

Report from the Journal on July 27th 1995.

the course on Wednesday as the greenkeepers battled to get the course back up to par.

● At the height of the storm two firecrews from Exmouth were called out after lightning set fire to gorse on the common near Woodbury Castle. For an hour in pouring rain and with lightning flashing all around them they brought the blaze under control.

Despite the downpour they had to use hose reels to extinguish the blaze. One of the crew said later: "It was very hairy with all the lightning coming down all around us."

●THE trail of destruction. *ref. 982/12a.*

... and to the Greens

Like the bunkers, the greens received much critical attention. For example, in 1988 the committee initiated "an onslaught against pitch marks". It was decided to obtain flags for each hole, bearing the appeal "Repair pitch marks" and to issue repair forks free to all players when they signed in for competitions.

There was discussion too on the merits of hand-driven motor cutters, which had the benefit of roller action, versus the Triplex machine and trials were carried out on the 11th green. A consensus was reached whereby the grass would be hand-cut in winter and partially so in summer, when it was cut four times a week. Worm casting was controlled by spraying with "Sydone" – which promised "to kill all known worms"!

Hollow tining continued to be carried out by a contractor about every two years. Double flags were placed on the 5th, 12th and 15th greens.

The approaches to the greens were also successfully treated. On one of his visits of inspection in 1983, Hamilton-Stutt noted "compaction" in front of many greens. The answer was a course of deep tining. When the irrigation system was updated in 1990 it was decided to extend its scope by providing water to the approaches of all the greens apart from the three short holes. Watermation undertook the work for £15,000.

At an AGM in 1992 members voted in favour of altcrations to thc 10th green. The apron in front was to be made much smaller, thereby enlarging the green itself. At the same time the lip of the cross bunker would be modified. This work was undertaken by the greens staff in the autumn.

In 1997 the recording of competition results was speeded up through the purchase of a Player Score Input computer program, priced at £1000.

Practice Ground

The idea of extending the practice ground below the 1st tee by leasing additional land was raised in 1983 but not pursued. Instead, the area was cleared of gorse to the east and west during 1984. An extra lower tee was added adjoining the existing one. To assist the work a "stone machine" was brought on site. It all cost about £1500.

In 1992 it was decided not to build a 9-hole course on the extra land leased from Clinton Devon Estates. An outline estimate had priced the scheme at about £250,000, not including stone clearance and infrastructure costs. So it was agreed to rent the major portion of the additional land to a local farmer and to create a new practice area out of the lower field which runs to the north of the 1st and 2nd holes and roughly parallel to the 4th. A path would be made through from the existing practice ground. The teeing area was placed at the foot of the slope for shots to be hit uphill. Planning permission was received in 1994.

In 1999 some effort was put in to establishing three or four holes on the perimeter of this area for use by the Professional when teaching or by members at other times. However, the potential hazard of both the practice holes and the driving range being in use at the same time made the scheme a difficult one to operate.

Taking Stock

In June 1986, for interest's sake, an analysis was made of the 374 full members of the club from the viewpoint of length of membership. The breakdown was:

127 joined since 1980
142 joined during the seventies
87 joined during the sixties
18 joined during the fifties
17 joined before that.

The figures show that:
- almost one third of the membership was 'new', of five years or less standing;
- there was an influx of members in the 1970s;
- the eighties were likely to bring in a larger number;
- 35 people – almost one tenth of the total – had been members for over 25 years.

Membership did, in fact, rise in the late 1980s, from 450 in 1988 to 470 in 1990.

Lost Treasure Found

In November 1987, presumably during a general tidy-up or clearing-out session, 75 volumes of the bound copies of the magazine Golf, and its successor Golf Illustrated, were discovered, dating from 1892 to the early 1920s. There were also some volumes of The Field from 1932 to 1933. Their value was recognised and expert advice taken. They eventually went to America, sold at auction for £13,300.

Clubhouse Extension

The feeling that the club needed more room was evidently present in 1985 but there was initial hesitation about exactly what form the expansion should take. At this time ideas centred on the ladies' accommodation, the kitchen and the greenkeepers' shed. Suitable improvements would cost about £24,000. It was also suggested that the men's east locker room could be turned into a Junior Club Room for about £500.

Ideas continued to be mulled over for another year. Plans were received in May 1986 that sketched how "more general space" could be achieved as well as allowing for "better arrangements for the ladies". The idea of a spike bar was discussed but quickly dropped and at this date too an extension to the bar and dining room was considered "a low priority" not to be proceeded with in the immediate future. Only on the urgent need to improve the ladies' accommodation was a decision made. The cost would be about £23,000 and the amount was found by the following measures:

- Subscriptions were raised by 10% instead of 5%.
- Thirty extra members were to be admitted.
- Thursday was to be set aside as a Society Day.
- Green fees were to be raised from £14 to £16.

It was not until January 1991 that the Buildings' Development Sub-committee agreed that "the essential requirement was to provide more space in the public rooms without in any way spoiling the essential character of the clubhouse". The design that was finally approved was that put forward by a firm of Torquay architects, Kay-Elliott. In December it was decided that a £10 levy should be incorporated into subscriptions to help fund the building programme.

In January 1992 the firm of R. J. and W. M. Sharland was awarded the building contract. As the building work went ahead plans were made for the interior decoration. The design concept and colour scheme were provided by Quay Design. Sufficient tables and chairs were purchased to seat ninety people in the dining area and thirty-six people in the lounge. The bar was refaced with mahogany panelling. The final costs were:

Building work	£54,500
Interior refurbishment	£28,000
Fees	£6,000
Terrace	£3,500
Total	£92,000

The extension was formally opened by Lord Clinton on 24th April 1992.

The Ladies' Locker Room

In November 1994 certain areas of the clubhouse were identified for improvement. These were: the ladies' locker room, a refurbished men's locker room, a new main entrance and a rearrangement of the office accommodation. Proposals prepared by the architects, Kay-Elliott, showed an estimated cost of £120,000, which could be funded by a £100 levy on each full member. By June 1995 the ladies had produced a list of requirements for the extension to their facilities and there was general agreement that they should have priority.

After much discussion on how extensive the proposed changes should be and whether other improvements – such as electrical rewiring – should be drawn into the scheme, an "Information Meeting" was held in the summer of 1996 which made it clear that the membership wanted a simple extension to the ladies changing room. In July, therefore, the Exmouth firm of Ian Howick and Associates was asked to draw up plans, which, when produced, had the whole-hearted support of the ladies. The cost, about £80,000, was to be met with a £35 levy on each full member. When approval had been given by an EGM in November, the contract, after tenders, was awarded to Sharlands in February 1997, the work to be completed within twelve weeks.

Display of Trophies

The enlargement of the clubhouse in 1992, with the consequent enjoyment of the smart new environment, encouraged the restoration of the collection of antique golf clubs which had been out of sight for some years. They were effectively lit and displayed in a cabinet to the right of the fireplace.

A year later a new trophy cabinet, costing £2000, was built into an archway facing the entrance doors to the bar. There the club's impressive collection of cups, bowls and salvers gleamed under the lights, together with statuettes and other sculptures, all testimony to the number of competitions organised in this busy and successful club

East Devon's teams playing in the Palairet Memorial Trophy continued the pattern of success of previous years by winning in 1987 and in 2000, the millennium year.

Major Repairs

As its centenary approached, the clubhouse inevitably showed signs of age and so a fairly constant programme of repairs had to be undertaken if it was to remain a pleasant environment in which to relax and a safe place in which to work. Among the major items were the rewiring of the electrical system, the updating of the Steward's flat and extensive work to the roof. The men's locker room went through several stages of refurbishing, including the installation of power-showers.

Some of these improvements were associated with implementing the Health and Safety at Work regulations. In June 1995 the club appointed a consultant to advise on these matters and also on employment policy. The surface of the yard outside the kitchen was repaired. Access to the cellar, which had been converted to a beer store and wine cellar, was improved by work on the steps and handrail. Fire drills were practised, with the aim of evacuating the building in under one minute. The recently donated ship's bell, which had been hung close to the bar to act as a Captain's bell for gaining the attention of members, was pressed into use as a fire alarm. The Stewardess's office was reorganised and a rest-room provided for the staff.

The former Ladies' Room – known for some time as the Function Room when the ladies became full members of the club and renamed the Pheasant Room in April 1998 – was given a 'face-lift' with new soft furnishings.

Both Golf Cottage (the Professional's house) and Chine Cottage (the Head Greenkeeper's house) underwent some modernisation before they were returned to the estate in 1986.

Social Events

By the 1980s film shows had seen their best days. The last screening was in 1983, when there was a showing of the 1980 US Masters. It was perhaps the difficulty of obtaining sufficiently interesting material that made this type of evening less attractive than before.

In the same way the evenings of carols gradually lost their appeal. The Christmas Draw and Carol Singing was an event taken seriously at the beginning of the 1980s, particularly the carol singing. Live music was provided, usually an organist, who, in 1980, charged £30 for the evening. Song sheets were handed round and the Christmas festivities got under way. Although the playing of the Peter Curtis Silver Ensemble was held to be "a splendid feature" of these occasions, support gradually dwindled and in 1990 the carol singing was cancelled.

Annual cocktail parties were no longer held regularly in the nineties and the Winter Foursomes Auction, begun in 1982, did not take place after 1994. Other diversions were tried. It was noticed that social events run in tandem with golf appeared to be particularly popular. The Friday golf and supper evenings usually began in May and ran through to the autumn at intervals of about six weeks. In June there was the "Midsummer Madness" competition: a shotgun start at 5.30 a.m., the best golf that one could manage, followed by a hearty breakfast. Versions of this type of entertainment were the Texas Scramble or Cross Country golf, followed by a barbecue and disco. In 1997 the club invested in its own gas barbecue for £800.

The annual club dance also continued. It was usually held at Bicton Gardens and was regularly enjoyed by about 130 members and guests. In 1987 there was a break with tradition when it was decided to hold a Summer Ball, with live music, in the clubhouse itself. The addition of a marquee meant that the number attending could rise to 200. For several years this worked very well. In

1991 there was a return to Bicton with the holding of a joint Ball with Sidmouth Golf Club. Prices for these dances gradually rose through the 1980s from £8 to £15 each. In the mid to late nineties the trend was to keep the Summer Ball or Party in-house. The purchase of a new dance floor in 1995 was good news for all the dancers in the club and that year it was put to good use at a very successful Summer Ball.

Supper dances with a theme dress code such as "the Roaring Twenties" or "the Sixties" and parties for Valentine's Day and Hallowe'en have proved great fun. Burns' Night was first introduced in 1995 and has always been well attended. Although the social scene is not attractive to everyone, the variety of occasions on offer ensures that as many as possible are drawn to the club to enjoy that great blessing, companionship, which has always been associated with the game of golf.

Club Diary

1995 was the year when it was decided to produce a combined diary and fixture list, together with a list of members and their telephone numbers. From that date it has proved its value in sorting out the schedules – golfing and social – of many of the club's members.

A New Constitution

In 1988 the Captain of the day proposed a new system for running affairs which, if adopted, would mean revising the existing constitution. The proposal was that a Management Committee should run the club while the Captain and his Committee should be responsible for running the golf and social activities. The idea received lukewarm support and was not pursued.

In September 1989, however, the scheme was again brought forward and later given more prominence with a visit, in January 1990, from a representative of the Association of Golf Club Secretaries which advocated implementing the two-tier system. A year later, in January 1991, an ad hoc committee was appointed "to consider the Club's present management structure and to recommend appropriate change". A summary of its findings was published for members' information. A meeting was then held in December 1991 to give members the opportunity to ask questions and state opinions. An Extraordinary General Meeting voted in favour of the change in January 1992.

It took some time for the change to be implemented as details had to be discussed, such as the composition of the committees. In 1992, for example, it was accepted that the Ladies' Captain should be a member of the Management Committee. In the same year, and therefore for the first time, both male and female members of East Devon elected a lady on to the Management Committee. Papers were drafted and redrafted and a new Rule Book, submitted to an AGM in 1993, was approved. From then on the club Captain chaired the Management Committee, from which were drawn five sub-committees: Finance, House, Green, Competitions and Handicaps, and the Captain's sub-committee.

Tied up with the creation of a two-tier system of management was the proposal to introduce the office of Chairman. This innovation was advocated in certain golfing circles such as the magazine The Golf Club Secretary, which, in April 1994, issued its long-awaited publication The Most Efficient Organisation for a Members' Golf Club. In July the committee set up a working party to consider the issue of appointing a Chairman and a month later ruled in favour. The procedure to elect the Chairman then had to be worked out, together with the division of responsibilities between the Captain and the Chairman. This was achieved, but in October the decision on whether to have a Chairman for the Management Committee was deferred until an EGM in January 1995.

At the EGM it was emphasised that the Chairman of the Management Committee was subordinate to the office of Captain, who remained the senior officer of the Club. It would still be the Captain's responsibility to nominate the chairmen of the sub-committees which reported to the Management Committee. The Chairman would stand for election – or re-election – at the AGM. Members voted in favour of creating the new office and from 1995 it was the Chairman, not the club Captain, who chaired meetings of the Management Committee.

In September 1997 the scheme to change to a "two-committee" structure was again proposed, having been turned down in committee the previous year. This time a paper was submitted to members at a "discussion meeting". The submission was approved but with the addition that the Captain and the Ladies' Captain should be full members of the Management Committee with the right to vote. With this alteration the change was successfully carried at an EGM in February 1998. The two-committee structure became operational in April.

In August of the same year it was agreed that the club Captain and the Ladies' Captain should both take office from 1 January each year.

The VAT Refund

In 1994 the Secretary and the club's auditor attended courses relating to VAT as it was applied to private members' clubs following a European Court ruling on the status of members" sports clubs. Shortly afterwards it was learned that a refund "in the region of £100,000" was due to the club in respect of VAT paid on members' subscriptions and entrance fees from 1990 to 1994. An EGM called in January 1995 to decide – among other questions – how this money should be used, voted in favour of returning it to the members. Each member's refund was calculated at 90 per cent of the total of VAT that he or she had been charged for subscriptions and/or entrance fees during that period.

The Introduction of the Swipe Card

As early as 1992 it was suggested by the House Sub-committee that the club should introduce a compulsory £50 levy which members could redeem by purchasing food and drink. The proposal, however, was not pursued until May 1997 when the Chairman of the Management Committee again raised the subject. On this occasion, additionally, the card was linked with security in that it would also be used to gain access to the clubhouse. It was acknowledged that the initial cost would be "fairly high", considering that new tills, a reader and door-entrance system would have to be provided. However, a demonstration was organised for November.

There the matter rested until August 1998. The scheme had been successfully introduced at other clubs and at one it was even reported to have increased bar and catering income by 50 per cent. It was felt that at East Devon swipe cards could be introduced by including "the bar levy" as part of the annual subscription. The average cost of various systems was £12,000.

In August 1999 the introduction of swipe cards was put to the members at an EGM and voted through.

And in Conclusion...

And so the modernisation programme continues. A refurbishment of the interior décor of the clubhouse is planned for Centenary Year. Other improvements will no doubt follow. It is an ongoing process.

Looking back over one hundred years of golf at East Devon certain features are clear. The architects of the course in 1899 started with – or deliberately chose – enormous advantages. The course was placed in a dominant position, from it were afforded superb scenic views, while the rise and fall of its land provided interest and variety.

To these natural advantages has been added human effort. A very great deal of care, close attention, anxious concern and knowledgeable effort have been expended – one might say lavished – on the land itself. The placing of the holes has been thoughtfully developed, the bunkers skilfully sighted and the greens nurtured. All this has been to one end – the provision of a real golfing challenge. It has been rightly said that East Devon is an exhilarating course.

Allied to the concentration on the course has been an awareness that the social side of golf is a valued adjunct to the game. The creation of an appealing clubhouse with the necessary amenities and a relaxing atmosphere has been the work of many people over the years.

This alliance of a distinguished course with a pleasant environment is a winning combination on which confidence in the future can be safely founded.

Appendix I

CAPTAINS, SECRETARIES AND PROFESSIONALS

East Devon Golf Club: Captains

1902	C. E. Pine-Coffin
1903/4	E. G. Williams
1905	S. R. Baker
1906	C. E. Pine-Coffin
1907/8	F. Cobbett
1909	F. J. C. Hunter
1910	Col. Burgmann
1911	W. Oxley
1912/13	S. H. Brierley
1914	F. J. C. Hunter
1915–17	W. H. Jarvis
1918/19	G. Simpson
1920	S. H. Brierley
1921	Brig. Gen. A. Martyn CB CMG
1922	Lt. Col. F. G. R. Ostrehan
1923	E. J. Spencer
1924	Maj. Gen. W. C. Black CSI CIE
1925	L. D. Thomas
1926	M. Godfrey
1927	Sir R. W. Burnet KCVO
1928	H. C. Bennett
1929	Lt. Col. J. B. MacFarlan DSO
1930	H. C. Bennett
1931	H. W. Adie
1932/3	W. G. Parkes-Davis
1934	L. D. Thomas
1935	H. C. Bennett
1936	J. G. Leathart MC
1937	Col. C. E. Bateman-Champain
1938	Rev. T. G. Shelmerdine
1939	Brig. Gen. H. Fargus CB CMG DSO
1940	Capt. H. B. Mulleneux CBE RN
1941	J. M. Macaulay
1942	F. Livesey
1943	Rev. G. L. A. Heslop
1944	J. M. Armitage
1945	H. C. Bennett
1946	Capt. H. B. Mulleneux CBE RN
1947	Brig. Gen. H. Fargus CB CMG DSO
1948	J. M. Armitage
1949	J. M. Macaulay
1950	A. Lawrence Folker
1951	Col. R. O. Bradley
1952	Sir Duncan G. Mackenzie KCIE
1953	Col. G. L. Brown DSO
1954	Lt. Col. T. Aveling MC TD
1955	R. H. Naish TD
1956	G. M. Peaker
1957/8	R. I. Edwards MC
1959	A. M. Mackintosh
1960	R. P. Bowie
1961	L. E. Kernick
1962	L. D. Payne
1963	V. C. Tong
1964	A. E. Blair MBE
1965	J. H. Trapnell MC
1966	W. F. Hamer
1967	H. G. Bainbridge
1968	Maj. J. H. Wyllie
1969	H. C. Hockley OBE
1970	R. G. L. Benzie
1971	C. G. Vasey
1972	Grp. Capt. G. H. Tebboth OBE
1973	E. H. D. Low
1974	R. W. T. Blake
1975	H. W. Stocker
1976	G. W. Moxon
1977	S. Reynolds
1978	G. H. Law
1979	F. J. Twiselton
1980	J. Berry
1981	R. C. Carter
1982	P. J. Menhenitt
1983	Maj. A. D. Parsons MBE MC
1984	A. D. Oag
1985	R. Greenaway
1986	P. Turnbull OBE TD
1987	G. A. Young
1988	J. M. MacCormick
1989	G. K. Baker
1990	A. H. Sage
1991	G. Baynham
1992	L. M. H. Fry
1993	R. J. Hall
1994	M. A. Yates

1995	P. S. Lilly
1996	N. Griffin
1997	J. J. B. Saul
1998	D. W. Watson
1999	A. M. R. Miller
2000	T. E. Heard
2001	R. G. Lankester
2002	R. Greenaway

East Devon Ladies Golf Club: Captains

1906	Miss Morant
1907/8	Mrs Baker
1909–16	Mrs Baker
1919	Miss Capel
1920–25	Mrs Hammond
1926–36	Mrs Mitford
1937–39	Miss V. Smith
1947–50	Miss P. Aplin
1951–53	Miss M. Foster
1954	Miss P. McIntosh
1955	Mrs E. Rigg
1956	Miss W. Marris
1957	Mrs Edwards
1958	Mrs E. Pursey
1959	Mrs S. L. Morris
1960	Mrs R. E. Lee
1961	Mrs S. L. Morris
1962	Mrs H. Blatcher
1963	Mrs Edwards
1964	Mrs G. G. Powell
1965	Mrs W. A. Kain
1966	Mrs E. M. Pursey
1967	Mrs J. Oliver
1968	Mrs R. E. Lee
1969	Mrs G. Curle
1970	Mrs D. Garrick
1971	Mrs J. R. L. Orange
1972	Mrs R. Twitchell
1973	Mrs S. M. Nankivell
1974	Mrs C. S. Davidson
1975	Mrs L. D. Payne
1976	Mrs M. G. Isard
1977	Mrs E. A. Calderbank
1978	Mrs H. A. Thomas
1979	Mrs G. R. Turnbull
1980	Mrs A. A. Slocock
1981	Mrs D. Oag
1982	Mrs H. L. Knight
1983	Mrs J. Berry
1984	Mrs E. B. James
1985	Mrs H. Coton
1986	Mrs T. Philp
1987	Mrs P. Tribble
1988	Mrs M. Edwards
1989	Mrs P. Hayes
1990	Mrs J. Miller
1991	Mrs L. Caldwell
1992	Mrs M. Onley

EDGC: Lady Captains

1992	Amalgamation
1992	Mrs M. Onley
1993	Mrs S. Wilde
1994	Mrs V. B. Freeman
1995	Mrs J. E. Benzie
1996	Mrs M. Tye
1997	Mrs M. D. Whitehead
1998	Mrs A. Smith
1999	Mrs M. J. Halton
2000	Mrs J. J. Hall
2001	Mrs H. Greenaway
2002	Mrs J. Miller

Secretaries of EDGC

1902–1905	J. Oliver
1905–1913	W. Whytock
1913–1914	R. C. N. Palairet
1914–1919	R. W. Friend
1919–1920	R. C. N. Palairet
1920–1926	L. H. Gay
1926–1944	C. Kitchin
1944–1947	P. F. F. Bourne
1947–1952	G. E. B. Honeyman
1952–1957	H. D. O'Lyle
1957–1960	W. H. C. Palmer
Jan.–June 1960	J. O. Wood
1960–1970	L. R. Allen
1970–1982	A. D. Mercer
1982–1984	C. J. Brewer
1984–1986	D. E. Matthews
1986–1989	R. S. B. Luckman
1989–1997	J. C. Tebbet
1997–	R. Burley

The three County Captains, (left) Roy Greenaway, (right) Harry Stocker (front) Mrs Bill James, in 1988.

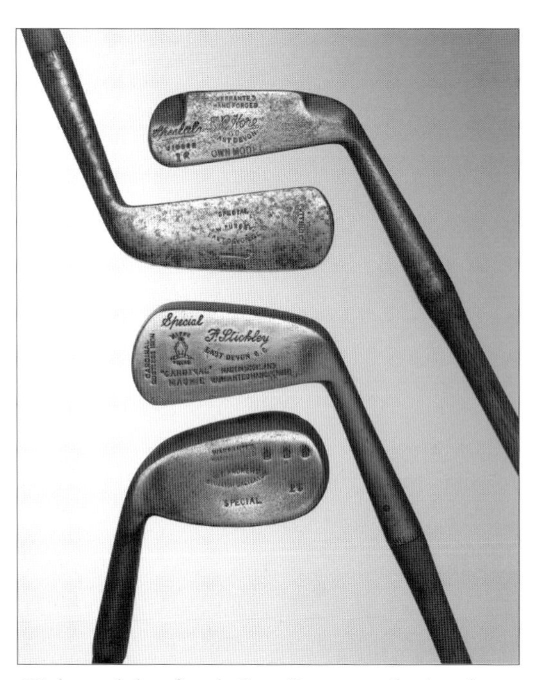

Hickory clubs of early East Devon professionals.

The Professionals

1902–04	L.J. Searle
1904–07	F. Pennington
1907–12	B. Andrews
1912–22	W. Pursey
1922–28	E. Hore
1928–44	F. Stickley
1945–75	A. Robins
1975–85	D. Howard
1985–present	T. Underwood

The first Professional engaged by the club in 1902 was L. J. Searle, a resident of Exmouth at that time, but in early 1904, it was felt that a more experienced Professional was required. Searle's career continued later at Beckenham Ladies (1907–22), Elmstead Sundridge Park (1922–30) and Eltham Warren into the 1930s.

His replacement in July 1904, from Royal Jersey, was F. Pennington, but from the outset he did not seem to be a good choice, as by October 1905 he was requiring members to pay their accounts monthly and to pay for balls by cash. His wages were sixteen shillings per week. The committee tried to help by drawing Chamier's attention in December 1904 "to the unsatisfactory conditions" under which he was working.

"He is greatly inconvenienced by having to go to and fro for his meals if he wishes to be properly fed. This is prejudicial to the interests of the Club. The building of the cottage should be proceeded with without delay."

The appeal worked. Golf Cottage – the home of the Professional until 1986 – was built in 1905. Pennington was asked to resign in July 1907 and appears as a Professional at Blundell Ainsdale in 1921, where he remained well into the 1930s.

He was succeeded by Brian Andrews from Westward Ho!, the job having been turned down by Ernest Kenyon, the Exmouth Professional. Andrews came with his son, highly recommended by Charles Gibson, and they were engaged for 18

117

Summary of Bills for the Building of Golf Cottage

1905		Payments	£	s	d
Page	100	Mechanics Labourers Wages	149	17	11
	103	Geo Hooper's Brick Bill	34	19	5
		Wm Thomas's Tile acct Chimney Pipes 23.8.9	19	8	2
		Hooper & Hookes Lias D 4.0.4	10	6	4½
	104	Devon Trading Company Rubble	2	2	6
		Heywood Cement	2	12	6
	113	Sharpe Bill for Timber	52	3	4
	111	Seagimoors " for Sills &c	6	3	1½
		Bennetts Bill for Iron Ladder	19	19	8
	117	Hermans Casting	1	4	0
	115	Sansoms "	16	11	
	117	Goslings "	7	13	0
		Paint & Colour	3	10	0
		Fences & Gates	6		
		Grates & Furnace	4	10	0
			331	1	0
		Entered account for Settee Land work as £	345	0	0

Golf Cottage cost sheet.

Above: Ernest Kenyon and Walter Pursey
Below: Stickley's original contract.

I AGREE to take the post of Professional to the East Devon Golf Club at a Salary of £100 per annum payable monthly (£8-6-8 per month from Monday, April 1st 1929).

I UNDERTAKE to devote my whole time to carrying out the usual duties of a Professional Golfer and the management of the shop and repairing and making clubs etc., the giving of lessons on the terms as agreed with the Club Secretary and to carry out any duties of a Golf Professional that he may direct.

I AM also responsible for the proper conduct of the men employed by me in the shop and in the event of their misdemeanour undertake to dismiss them at one month's notice if required by the Club Secretary.

I MAY take three weeks' leave per annum, and may take one day per week off duty with reasonable leave to play in Golf Tournaments, all leave to be subject to the Secretary's approval as to dates.

I MAY close the shop daily at 6 p.m.

MY EMPLOYMENT may be terminated at any time by two months' notice given by me to, or received by me from, the Secretary.

________ 1929. F Stickley

shillings per week. Andrews had been Professional to Westward Ho! Ladies from 1904–07. A similar story to that of the previous Professional appears to have taken place, since by August 1911 the Secretary was reporting unsatisfactory maintenance of workshop and supervision of caddies by Andrews, and by July 1912 he was requested to resign.

Kenyon was again mentioned as a possible successor but Walter Pursey, who had been Andrews' assistant, was given a three-month trial at 12s.6d. per week. Walter Pursey remained at the club until 1922, then moved to Seattle, following some involvement with a lady member! UK golf records state that he retired through ill health; however, amongst his medals were the Washington State Open Championships for 1926 and 1928, and the Washington P.G.A. Championships for 1929 and 1930, so this must have been far from the true story. His wife Enid presented the Pursey Cup in the 1960s, which is still played for.

He was succeeded at East Devon by Ernie Hore from Axecliff, who remained until 1928.

Hore's successor was Freddie Stickley, Professional at Stoneham (1922–23) and Royal Guernsey (1925–28). Stickley's original contract makes interesting reading. He was a good golfer and prolific clubmaker. He qualified for the Open Championship in 1932, set a new East Devon course record of 66 on 3rd August 1934, and was Devon matchplay champion in 1936. By 1941 Stickley was forty-six years old and became a sergeant and section commander in the Home Guard. His wages at this time had risen to £100 as Professional,

Above: Dunlop Trophy to commemorate the course record of F Stickley in 1934.
Below: Close-up of commemorative panel.

£78 as Caddie master and £150 as Steward, with his wife, plus free housing, fuel, light and food. Freddie Stickley was obviously a good servant to the club, so when he became seriously ill in 1943 with cancer and then died in February 1945, it was agreed that Mrs Stickley should carry on as Professional and Caddie master, and that Owen Stickley, their son, should be considered for the Professional's job on his return home from serving in the RAF. This did not work out successfully and the position was offered to Arthur Robins in December 1945.

Arthur Robins was brought up at Moorlands Farm, the only house at that time between what is now Links Road and Lansdowne Road. He came to the club as a caddie during the First World War and was later assistant to Hore and Stickley for twelve years before becoming the Professional at Tavistock in 1938. During this period he was Devon Champion from 1931 to 1934. His salary was £150 per annum plus the tenancy of Golf Cottage. He became a much liked Professional and was most proficient at tailoring clubs to fit individual players. Tragically, his seven-year-old son, having walked across the course, was killed in a fall from the clifftop while searching for birds' eggs. To mark Robins' retire-

Arthur Robins on far left beside Sir John H. Amory with Scratch Bennett of East Devon on far right, c.1930.

Arthur & Mrs Robins (centre) being presented with retirement Rose Bowl watched by Harry Stocker (left) 1974.

ment in 1975, sixty teams from Devon, Cornwall and Somerset took part in a Testimonial Competition organised at East Devon.

Robins was succeeded in 1975 by David Howard, who remained at the club until 1985.

Trevor Underwood, our current Professional, came to East Devon from Ryde Golf Club at the age of twenty-five and has served the club well to the present day.

Appendix II

WINNERS OF DEVON COUNTY TROPHIES

Devon County Golf Union: Individual Honours

Devon Amateur Championship

1930	F. H. Carroll
1983–1991	A. Richards
1986	P. M. Newcombe

Gold Medal

1912/1913	C. C. Aylmer
1935	J. K. MacFarlan
1986	P. M. Newcombe

Devon Salver

1982/1986/1987	P. M. Newcombe
1991/1996/1997	P. M. Newcombe

Devon Challenge Cup

1973	M. J. Baker

Presidents Trophy

1991	T. Gorfin
1996	R. Martin
1999	G. Harper

Wish Slater Trophy

1974	R. W. T. Blake
1980/1995	P. M. Newcombe
1997	G. Harper

Cooper Cup
1973 R. G. L. Benzie
1998 G. Harper

Goodban Cup
1987–1989 P. M. Newcombe
2000 K. Harper

Western Morning News Cup
1973 R. Greenaway

Devon Handicap Cup
1987 P. M. Newcombe
1995 J. Smith

Reynolds Salver
1996 P. M. Newcombe

Gray Memorial Trophy
1996 P. M. Newcombe

Goldsmith Salver
1971 R. W. T. Blake & F. Twiselton
1987 G. K. Baker & P. M. Newcombe

Goldsmith Salver Ind. Stableford
1995 G. L. M. Benzie

Seniors Scratch Championships
1996 B. Devetta
1999 T. Heard

Dartmouth Trophy (Over 35s)
1996 R. Martin
2001 P. M. Newcombe

Brockman Trophy (Youth Champion)
1980/1981/1984/ P. M. Newcombe

Andrew Trophy (Junior Champion)
1979/1980 P. M. Newcombe
1997 G. Harper
2000 D. Crookall

Keith Abraham Cup (Juniors Om)
1998/1999 K Harper

Torbay Country Golf Club Cup
1971 R. W. T. Blake & F. Twiselton

Devon County Golf Union: Club Team Honours

Palairet Memorial Trophy
1968/1969/1970/1971/1987/2000

Club Team Challenge Cup
1928/1935/1980/1985/1991/1993

Horsley Cup (2nd Palairet)
1934/1967

Inter Club Scratch Foursomes
1938/1987/1994/1996

Brown Cup (3rd Palairet)
1980/1995

Inter Club Handicap Foursomes
1971/1986/1991

Lake Trophy (4th Palairet)
1988/1991/1999

Brockman Cup
1973

Juniors

Basil Steer Trophy
1990

Two Successful Players

In recent years two of East Devon's most successful golfers have been Paul Newcombe and Katie Tebbet.

In 1978, at the age of fifteen, Paul returned an "incredible" score of 64 to break the club record. At that time it was the lowest ever gross score on any Devon course. For this feat Peter Alliss gave him a generous mention in his book The Good Golf Guide of 1986. The club presented him with a silver salver.

Paul was a member of the Devon team that won the English Amateur and English County Championship in 1985. He has won six Devon Salvers in all, three of them in the 1990s, and continues to play for the county team. As well as winning many club trophies, Paul has made numerous appearances in Palairet teams.

At national level, Katie won the English Ladies Stroke Play Championship and the English Ladies Under 23 Championship in 1990. She was also an England international.

In Devon, she was the Ladies County Champion from 1991 to 1994, and was also a committed member of the club's Still Cup team in the 1990s. (*See colour section page 69.*)

Devon County Ladies Golf Association: Honours for EDGC Ladies

DCLGA County Captains

1933–35 Mrs B. G. Bennett
1939 Mrs J. H. Foster
1946 Mrs B. G. Bennett
1988–1989 Mrs Bill James
2000–2001 Mrs Betty Baynham

County Champions (Championship Bowl)
Presented 1922
1939 Miss M. Foster (East Devon & Westward Ho!)
1950, 1952, 1953, 1954, 1960, 1965, 1966
Mrs M. Anstey (East Devon & Exeter)
1990–1994 Miss K. Tebbet

County Medal Final Cup (commenced 1962)
1984 Mrs A. Pagliero
1988 Mrs B. Baynham

Phyllis Collett Memorial Bowl (presented 1933)
(36 holes Handicap at Silver Division Meeting)
1964 Mrs R. Hellyer–Jones
1968 Mrs M. Anstey

(36 holes Handicap in Qualifying Round for Championship)
1984 Mrs S. Nankivell

The Gold Medal (presented 1922)
(36-hole Scratch Qualifying Competition for Championship)
1966–1968 Mrs M. Anstey

Jose Bruce Trophy (presented 1986)
1991–1995 Miss K. Tebbet

Coronation Cup (presented 1937)
(Runner-up to the Champion)
1981 Mrs P. Powell
1996 Miss S. Joll

Devon County Golf Club Scratch Cup
(origin and early use unknown)
1998–1999 Mrs S. Fowler

Bronze Scratch Cup – 1961
1966 Mrs A. Stanley
1991 Mrs L. Longmuir

Bronze Handicap Cup – 1961
1962 Mrs M. Tong
1983 Mrs T. Philp

County Bronze Division Meeting Scratch & Handicap
1962 Miss M. Stamp – Scratch & Miss W. Stamp – Handicap
1982 Mrs M. Wood – Scratch
1987 Mrs S. Fowler – Scratch & Handicap
1990 Mrs M. Heard – Scratch
1991 Mrs L. Down – Scratch & Handicap
1995 Mrs C. Rustom – Handicap
1996 Mrs P. Taylor – Handicap
1997 Mrs M. Archdeacon – Scratch & Handicap

Bronze Coronation Medal (presented 1929)
1962 Mrs M. Tong
1991 Mrs L. Down
1996 Mrs P. Taylor

Western Morning News Cup (presented 1936)
1938 East Devon
1974 East Devon (North & East)
1988 East Devon

Warren Crocus Salvers (commenced 1979)
1996 Mrs D. Brittain – Silver Division Salver

Express & Echo Shield (commenced 1985)
1993 Mrs M. Onley & Mrs J. Hall

E. Young Bowl (presented 1948)
1961 Mrs P. Powell
1964 Mrs P. Powell
1965/1966 Mrs M. Anstey
(Abandoned in 1968)

The Still Cup Challenge Trophy (commenced 1903)
(Inter Club Team Match-Play Scratch Competition)
East Devon won this trophy in: 1904, 1926, 1927, 1930, 1932, 1968, 1969, 1972, 1991, 1992, 1993.

E. Young Bowl Runner-up Still Cup from 1968. East Devon 1976, 1990, 1994.

Sheelah Creasy Bowl (presented in 1954)
(an Inter Club Team Match-Play Handicap Competition from 1966)
East Devon won this trophy in: 1967, 1979, 1987, 1989, 1992.

Olwen Williams Salver (presented in 1967)
(Runner-up Trophy to the Sheelah Creasy Bowl)
East Devon won this trophy in: 1980, 1984, 1990.

Doris Willes-Little Cup (presented in 1947)
(Inter Club Foursomes – Nominated Knockout)
Won by East Devon in:
1948/49 Miss E.M. Crothers/Miss M Foster
1952 Miss E.M. Crothers/Miss M.M. Stamp
1956 Mrs E.M. Pursey (née Crothers)/Miss M. Foster
1986 Mrs J.E. Miller/Mrs V.B. Freeman

Doris Willes-Little Runner-up Trophy (presented in 1949)
Won by East Devon in 1958

Lloyd-Williams Salver (presented 1934)
1964 Mrs R. Hellyer-Jones
1972 Mrs S. Nankivell
1985 Mrs J. Miller
1989 Mrs P. Hayes

Coronation Medal (presented 1902)
1963 Mrs V. Felce
1966 Mrs P. Hellyer-Jones
1968 Mrs A. E. Randall
1971 Mrs I. P. Stephens
1972 Mrs M. G. Isard
1977 Mrs M. Onley
1981 Mrs R. Heale
1985 Mrs J. Miller
1993 Miss S. Joll

Stella Temple Memorial Cup (presented 1920)
(18-hole Scratch Cup)
1926 G. E. Hamilton
1961–1962 Mrs P. Powell
1966–1968 Mrs M. Anstey
1973 Mrs M. Isard

Scratch Runner-up Cup (presented in 1979 by DCLGA)
(Commemorating Chairmanship of ELGA of Mrs Joan Mackenzie)
1993 Miss S. Joll

Joan Mackenzie Salver (presented in 1983)
1981 Mrs R. E. Heale
1985 Mrs J. Miller
1993 Miss S. Joll

Appendix III

Winners of Major Club Competitions

ROLLE CUP – MEDAL
1902 S. R. Baker
1903 S. R. Baker
1904 C. E. Pine-Coffin
1905 E. Oliver
1906 E. Oliver
1907 F. J. C. Hunter
1908 H. C. Tringham
1909 F. Cobbett
1910 E. J. R-Rowe
1911 Capt. Goodwin
1912 Col. Barton
1913 H. K. Fulton
1914 No competition
1915 No competition

1916	No competition
1917	No competition
1918	No competition
1919	A. R. Walker
1920	H. Boden
1921	F. A. Dene
1922	W. G. Black
1923	M. Godfrey
1924	Col. Armytage
1925	Maj. Sutherland
1926	Col. Baldwin
1927	H. E. Wilson
1928	T. Cook
1929	Lt. Col. Macfarlan
1930	S. E. Langmore
1931	R. E. Lee
1932	V. K. Voss
1933	F. W. Lyon
1934	S. Couper
1935	Dr F. W. Morsden
1936	R. E. Lee
1937	R. E. Lee
1938	E. A. Rigg
1939	J. M. Armitage
1940	Brig. H. T. Dobbin CBE
1941	H. C. Bennett
1942	J. M. Macauley
1943	No competition
1944	No competition
1945	No competition
1946	No competition
1947	No competition
1948	D. B. Smith
1949	H. Rex
1950	H. Rex
1951	R. E. Lee
1952	H. T. Dixon
1953	C. A. Norris
1954	W. K. H. Coxe
1955	J. H. Higson
1956	A. J. Abbott
1957	W. Parry
1958	H. A. Harrison
1959	C. A. Norris
1960	H. Bainbridge
1961	A. E. Blair
1962	A. J. Abbott
1963	K. L. Trott
1964	J. H. Wyllie
1965	F. Jones
1966	J. B. Arrand
1967	C. E. D. Marker
1968	J. A. Bamsey
1969	C. S. Davidson
1970	F. J. Twiselton
1971	R. Greenaway
1972	A. L. Pratt
1973	N. Abraham
1974	A. Moxon
1975	A. Moxon
1976	P. Newcombe
1977	R. A. Gray
1978	M. Beal
1979	R. Troake
1980	C. K. Iles
1981	C. I. Hughes
1982	N. Richards
1983	S. P. Sturman
1984	G. H. Tebboth
1985	M. E. Whitelock
1986	D. E. Pagliero
1987	D. Bidmead
1988	C. Tyacke
1989	D. Allen
1990	P. Corney
1991	J. Rowbotham
1992	B. Sandrey
1993	J. Bewley
1994	R. Martin
1995	A. Holding
1996	P. Murray
1997	N. Surman
1998	J. M. Rowbotham
1999	S. Fereday
2000	R. J. Hollingworth
2001	M. Elstub

PINE-COFFIN CUP – STABLEFORD

1902	E. G. Williams
1903	S. R. Baker
1904	S. R. Baker
1905	S. R. Baker
1906	A. Crawford
1907	H. S. Ellis
1908	H. D. Were
1909	S. R. Baker
1910	F. B. Coppin
1911	T. A. Oliver
1912	J. H. Lightbody
1913	C. H. Minshall

1914	No competition
1915	No competition
1916	No competition
1917	No competition
1918	No competition
1919	O. C. Bristowe
1920	D. Grant
1921	H. Boden
1922	W. J. Warn
1923	C. W. H. Pulford
1924	J. W. Slaughter
1925	P. A. Parks Smith
1926	Lt. Col. G. Armitage
1927	T. Cook
1928	J. K. Macfarlan
1929	Maj. W. W. Meldon
1930	Maj. L. E. Dennys
1931	Dr A. M. Roome
1932	H. C. Bennett
1933	J. R. Burnett
1934	Col. C. E. Bateman-Champain
1935	F. H. Carroll
1936	H. Gardner
1937	A. E. Jennings
1938	V. K. Voss
1939	V. K. Voss
1940	Rev. T. G. Shelmerdine
1941	J. H. Higson
1942	Rev. T. G. Shelmerdine
1943	No competition
1944	No competition
1945	No competition
1946	No competition
1947	No competition
1948	J. M. Armitage
1949	R. J. Bayliss
1950	Lt. Col. T. Aveling
1951	Col. G. L. Brown
1952	J. W. Bingham
1953	R. H. Naish
1954	K. D. Jackson
1955	K. D. Jackson
1956	R. H. Naish
1957	J. Duxbury
1958	H. Gillingham
1959	R. H. Naish
1960	Col. H. R. Bird
1961	J. D. A. Cameron
1962	J. B. Arrand
1963	J. H. Trapnell
1964	D. S. Macdonald
1965	J. B. Arrand
1966	E. F. G. Lambert
1967	D. S. Macdonald
1968	W. A. Kain
1969	D. W. Soughton
1970	E. Low
1971	N. Richards
1972	J. Wingate
1973	W. H. Clarke
1974	R. W. T. Blake
1975	N. Richards
1976	R. W. T. Blake
1977	G. Needham
1978	R. Troake
1979	P. J. Menhenitt
1980	N. Richards
1981	J. Bradford
1982	R. Green
1983	J. W. Bradford
1984	J. L. Taylor
1985	D. E. Pagliero
1986	J. L. W. Legg
1987	R. E. Squire
1988	J. R. Clarke
1989	A. W. P. Stephens
1990	G. Benzie
1991	M. Mears
1992	T. E. Heard
1993	D. Everett
1994	A. J. Hawkins
1995	D. Everett
1996	S. Harrison
1997	J. Hall
1998	C. G. Bennett
1999	T. Ward
2000	J. .P Turnbull
2001	E. James

BANFIELD TROPHY – SCRATCH

1966	J. H. Wyllie
1967	J. H. Wyllie
1968	R. G. L. Benzie
1969	R. G. L. Benzie
1970	C. E. D. Marker
1971	C. E. D. Marker
1972	C. E. D. Marker
1973	J. H. Wyllie
1974	J. H. Wyllie
1975	N. Abraham

1976 P. J. Menhenitt
1977 R. Greenaway
1978 G. T. Page
1979 P. M. Newcombe
1980 P. M. Newcombe
1981 A. G. Morgan
1982 K. A. Murray
1983 K. A. Murray
1984 P. M. Newcombe
1985 A. D. Howard
1986 P. M. Newcombe
1987 R. Greenaway
1988 P. M. Newcombe
1989 B. Devetta
1990 P. M. Newcombe
1991 P. M. Newcombe
1992 P. M. Newcombe
1993 P. Sweeney
1994 B. Devetta
1995 P. M. Newcombe
1996 P. M. Newcombe
1997 P. M. Newcombe
1998 P. M. Newcombe
1999 P. M. Newcombe
2000 D. M. Crookall
2001 K. Harper

Winners of Major Club Competitions: Ladies

Ladies Bennett Cup

1950 Miss Goodwin
1951 Miss E. M. Crothers
1952 Mrs R. E. Lee
1953 Miss M. M. Stamp
1954 Mrs E. Rigg
1955 Mrs A. E. Engelbach
1956 Miss M. Foster
1957 Miss E. M. Pursey

Ladies Pursey Cup

1958 Mrs R, E. Lee
1959/60 Mrs W. L. Risden
1961–63 Miss M. Foster
1964 Mrs V. Felee
1965 Mrs M. Anstey
1966 Mrs K. M. Law
1967 Mrs W. H. Clarke
1968 Mrs R. Baker-Beall
1969 Mrs G. G. Powell
1970 Mrs J. R. L. Orange
1971 Mrs K. M. Law
1972 Mrs S. M. Nankivell
1973 Mrs M. S. Anstey
1974 Mrs J. R. L. Orange
1975 Mrs J. B. Cobb
1976 Mrs P. Powell
1977 Mrs J. R. L. Orange
1978 Mrs P. Tribble
1979 Mrs V. Freeman
1980 Mrs L. Parsons
1981 Mrs M. Edwards
1982 Mrs A. Slocock
1983 Mrs C. Bagnall
1984 Mrs V. Freeman
1985 Miss D. Bloomfield
1986 Mrs C. Bagnall
1987 Mrs M. Menhenitt
1988 Mrs M. Christie
1989 Mrs P. Hayes
1990 Mrs M. Tye
1991 Miss K. Tebbett
1992 Mrs E. Hunt
1993 Mrs J. Miller
1994 Mrs S. Meherne
1995 Mrs A. Corney
1996 Mrs R. Pratt
1997 Miss E. Cameron
1998/9 Mrs A. Corney
2000 Mrs E. Hunt
2001 Mrs H. Greenaway

Ladies Championship

1987 Miss J. Nelson
1988 Mrs J. Miller
1989 Miss S. V. Joll
1990 Miss K. Tebbet
1991 Miss J. Bell
1992–95 Miss K. Tebbet
1996 Mrs H. Greenaway
1997 Miss E. Cameron
1998 Mrs D. Brittain
1999–2001 Miss S. V. Joll

Bennett Cup (Scratch)

1999 Mrs H. Greenaway
2000 Mrs J. O. Lee
2001 Miss S. V. Joll

Appendix IV

COURSE RECORDS

Over a span of one hundred years it is natural that both the layout of the course and its yardage have changed a number of times. As a consequence it has been possible to set a new course record after each major change.

The first record holder that we know of was C. C. Aylmer of Sidmouth, a member at East Devon, who set a score of 71 prior to 1908.

In 1911 the amateur record was held by the club's Secretary, W. Whytock, with a round of 75. The Professional record was set by J. H. Taylor, with a 74.

A trophy was presented to commemorate a 66 by the then Professional at East Devon, Freddie Stickley, on 6th June 1934.

In 1961 the club Captain, R. P. Bowie, in his year of office, held the record with a round of 69.

The year 1978 saw Paul Newcombe go round in 64 and he again held the record in 1985, with a 68, after some remodelling of the course had been carried out. This was lowered to 65 by Roger Winchester in 1987.

It was then captured by Bob Martin in 1992, who went round in 65. This has recently been reclaimed by Paul Newcombe in July 2001 with a magnificent 61.Paul Newcombe, the club's Head Greenkeeper, got his timing right as the new record came within days of the final manuscript of this book being sent off to the publisher. His playing companions who

COMPETITION JULY MEDAL — DATE 25·7·92 — TIME 12 35

		Handicap	Strokes Rec'd	Please indicate which tee used.
Player A	R MARTIN·	4	4	PAR 70 SSS 70
Player B	S JACKSON			PAR 70 SSS 68
Player C				PAR 72 SSS 73

Hole	Marker's Score	White Yards	Par	Yellow Yards	Stroke Index	Score A	Score B	Score C	W =+ L = - H = 0 Points	Red Yards	Par	Stroke Index
1		348	4	330	15	3				302	4	15
2		342	4	338	13	3				294	4	13
3		414	4	371	1	4				405	5	3
4		142	3	113	17	3				124	3	17
5		363	4	350	7	4				331	4	7
6		526	5	477	11	3				466	5	11
7		392	4	374	3	4				352	4	1
8		207	3	189	9	3				192	3	9
9		469	4	451	5	5				437	4	5
OUT		3203	35	2993		32				2903	36	
PLEASE AVOID SLOW PLAY AT ALL TIMES												
10		150	3	142	16	3				138	3	16
11		335	4	319	10	3				290	4	10
12		486	5	478	4	5				465	5	2
13		145	3	128	18	3				122	3	18
14		411	4	381	2	4				381	4	4
15		308	4	301	12	4				295	4	12
16		406	4	377	8	3				364	4	8
17		455	4	444	6	4				414	5	6
18		340	4	327	14	4				312	4	14
IN		3036	35	2897		33				2781	36	
OUT		3203	35	2993		32				2903	36	
TOTAL		6239	70	5890		65				5684	72	

STABLEFORD POINTS OR PAR RESULT — HANDICAP 4 — NETT 61

Holes won .... Holes lost .... Result ....

Copyright Eagle Promotions Ltd 01883-344244

Markers Signature .... Players Signature ....

1992 course record card for R. Martin.

East Devon Golf Club

Marker's score	Hole No.	White tees yards	Yellow tees yards	Par	Stroke index	Gross score A	Gross score B	(Best) nett score	W + L – HO points
	1	343	327	4		4			
	2	341	338	4		3			
	3	414	370	4		5			
	4	151	122	3		3			
	5	361	347	4		5			
	6	524	476	5		4			
	7	392	380	4		5			
	8	206	189	3		3			
	9	464	447	4		3			
	Out	3196	2996	35		35			

Marker's score	Hole No.	White tees yards	Yellow tees yards	Par	Stroke index	Gross score A	Gross score B	(Best) nett score
	10	155	154	3		2		
	11	337	327	4		3		
	12	483	476	5		4		
	13	143	128	3		3		
	14	404	374	4		3		
	15	301	295	4		3		
	16	402	376	4		3		
	17	453	441	4		4		
	18	340	330	4		4		
	In	3018	2901	35		29		
	Out	3196	2996	35		35		
	Total	6214	5897	70		64		

Competition: BRITISH HEART FOUNDATION PRO AM   Date: 12 8 90

Player	course played white/yellow	H'cap	Strokes
A	GEORGE RYALL		
B			

Standard scratch score: white tees 70, yellow tees 68

H'cap / Net score / points

Marker's signature: [illegible]

Player's signature: [illegible]

Above: Current professional course record card for George Ryall. Below: Course record card for Roger Winchester.

East Devon Golf Club

AMATEUR COURSE RECORD

Marker's score	Hole No.	White tees yards	Yellow tees yards	Par	Stroke index	Gross score A	Gross score B	(Best) nett score	W + L – HO points
	1	343	327	4	15	3			
	2	341	338	4	13	4			
	3	414	370	4	3	4			
	4	151	122	3	17	2			
	5	361	347	4	7	3			
	6	524	476	5	11	5			
	7	392	380	4	1	4			
	8	206	189	3	9	3			
	9	464	447	4	5	5			
	Out	3196	2996	35		33			

Marker's score	Hole No.	White tees yards	Yellow tees yards	Par	Stroke index	Gross score A	Gross score B	(Best) nett score
	10	155	154	3	16	2		
	11	337	327	4	10	4		
	12	483	476	5	2	4		
	13	143	128	3	18	2		
	14	404	374	4	4	3		
	15	301	295	4	12	4		
	16	402	376	4	8	5		
	17	453	441	4	6	5		
	18	340	330	4	14	3		
	In	3018	2901	35		32		
	Out	3196	2996	35		33		
	Total	6214	5897	70		65		

Competition: CAPTAIN'S DAY   Date: 25 JULY 1987

Player	course played white/yellow	H'cap	Strokes
A	Roger Winchester		
B			

Standard scratch score: white tees 70, yellow tees 68

H'cap / Net score / points

Marker's signature: [illegible]

Player's signature: R. Winchester

East Devon course record smashed

● PAR EXCELLENCE! East Devon Golf Club member Paul Newcombe is a cut above the rest after breaking the course record for the SECOND time.

Paul (37), lopped three shots off the record in a Saturday competition as he went round in a nine-under par 61.

The first time he broke the record was as a 15-year-old in 1978, although since then the course has been lengthened.

Picture by Simon Horn (Ref: 1803/22)

EAST Devon Golf Club green-keeper Paul Newcombe showed just how well he knew his way around his own fairways as he smashed the course record during the monthly stableford competition.

Paul, who is 37, knocked three shots off the course record held by Sidmouth professional Roger Winchester as he went round in a nine-under par 61.

It is the second time Paul has broken the course record – although the last time was when he was just 15!

On that occasion he broke the previous record held by former professional and now commentator Peter Allis.

Paul raced through the first nine holes in a two-under 33, but didn't give much thought to the record until he was well on his way down the back nine. "I birdied the 13th to go five under and realised then it might be on," said Paul.

"I thought if I could stay focused I would have a really good chance of doing it, although not by quite so many.

Paul stormed down the back nine in 28 strokes – helped by six consecutive birdies and seven in total over eight holes.

Club professional Trevor Underwood said: "What an achievement – well done Paul!"

And East Devon Golf Club secretary Bob Burley was equally impressed, describing the round as "absolutely stupendous."

Extract from the Budleigh Salterton Journal, Thursday July 19, 2001

witnessed this amazing round of golf were Barry Devetta and Bill Wentworth, who marked his card. The current professional record is held by George Ryall, with a 64 in 1990.

Long Driving

The following details have been extracted from The Golfer's Companion, edited by Peter Lawless, 1937.

NEW COURSE RECORD

COMPETITION	DATE 14.7.01 / TIME 12.21	Handicap	Strokes Rec'd	Please indicate which tee used.
JULY STABLEFORD				
Player A PAUL NEWCOMBE		2		PAR 70 SSS 70 ✓
Player B BILL WENTWORTH				PAR 70 SSS 68
Player C				PAR 72 SSS 73

Hole	Marker's Score	White Yards	Par	Yellow Yards	Stroke Index	Score A	Score B	Score C	W = + L = - H = O Points	Red Yards	Par	Stroke Index
1		348	4	330	15	4			2	302	4	15
2		342	4	338	13	4			2	294	4	13
3		414	4	371	1	4			3	405	5	3
4		142	3	113	17	3			2	124	3	17
5		363	4	350	7	3			3	331	4	7
6		526	5	477	11	4			3	466	5	11
7		392	4	374	3	5			1	352	4	1
8		207	3	189	9	2			3	192	3	9
9		469	4	451	5	4			2	437	4	5
	OUT	3203	35	2993		33			21	2903	36	
PLEASE AVOID SLOW PLAY AT ALL TIMES												
10		150	3	142	16	3			2	138	3	16
11		335	4	319	10	3			3	290	4	10
12		486	5	478	4	4			3	465	5	2
13		145	3	128	18	2			3	122	3	18
14		411	4	381	2	3			4	381	4	4
15		308	4	301	12	3			3	295	4	12
16		406	4	377	8	3			3	364	4	8
17		455	4	444	6	4			2	414	5	6
18		340	4	327	14	3			3	312	4	14
	IN	3036	35	2897		28			26	2781	36	
	OUT	3203	35	2993		33			21	2903	36	
	TOTAL	6239	70	5890		61			47	5684	72	

STABLEFORD POINTS OR PAR RESULT — HANDICAP — NETT

Holes won .... Holes lost .... Result ....

Copyright Eagle Promotions Ltd 01883-344244

Markers Signature W. WENTWORTH   Players Signature PAUL NEWCOMBE.

Paul Newcombe's new course record card.

"In September 1934 over the East Devon Course, Budleigh Salterton, Mr T. H. V. Haydon, Royal Wimbledon, did the following drives, certified over the signatures of two members of the East Devon Club:

1. Drove to the edge of the ninth green, 456 yards downhill.
2. Overdrove the eleventh, 358 yards dogleg.
3. Drove just short of the seventeenth green, 450 yards."

Appendix V

Budleigh Town Golf Club

The origins of the Town Club go back to the summer of 1910 when several of the local trades-men approached Andrews, the club Professional, about the possibility of being allowed to play golf in the evenings. It appears that the Exmouth links had such an arrangement at that time. The Secretary, Whytock, was quite in favour as the course was "practically free of members after 5 p.m." and he did not think many tradesmen would play. Chamier responded by writing to the Secretary of Bude Golf Club for the conditions applying to its Town Club.

A year later, however, in spring 1911, it emerged that the "feeling of the Club's Committee" was against the proposal. It was rejected on the grounds that the course was "already sufficiently crowded" and besides, could not the tradesmen "use some spare ground on the other side of the Otter"? Alternatively, perhaps Lord Clinton could be asked to "re-make the nine holes in Otterton Park's former golf course".

The Tradesmen's Association then appealed by letter to Lord Clinton, who thought they "should be able to use the course on certain days at certain seasons", though not when it was busy. This view was presented at the Annual General Meeting of 1912 and was once again rejected. Lord Clinton expressed his "disappointment" and asked the club's committee to draw up some more detailed proposals that could be resubmitted to members. He felt that the right to play some golf would be "a great boon" to the artisans.

Rules

By September 1912 his wishes had prevailed. A set of rules was drawn up, the main points were:

- Membership to be limited to 20.
- All members to be resident in Budleigh Salterton and engaged in trade or business there.
- Hours of play: every Thursday and Saturday from 2 p.m. to dusk, every other weekday from 5 p.m. to dusk except during Easter week, club meetings and at any other time by notice.
- A subscription of 10s.6d. to be paid (half the club subscription at that time).
- The privileges granted were "dependent upon its being found that their enjoyment does not interfere with the convenience of the members of the East Devon Golf Club and are liable to be cancelled at one month's notice".

Formation

The Town Club was then formed on 26th April 1913, with a handful of members. One of the original promoters of the scheme, Mr Shand, the Salterton pharmacist, assumed the role of Secretary, one which he held for many years. At this time arrangements were casual. With so few members there may not have been a need for formal meetings. When, in 1919, the main club doubled the artisans' subscription but halved the number of them allowed to play no protest was made because "the number desirous of joining the Town Club was less than ten". Those who did play were bank clerks, the town's surveyor, the town clerk and the Gas Board's manager. There were one or two lady members. Initially, no competitions were organised. By the 1930s, however, many more people wished to join and so the original maximum of twenty players was re-established.

A further impetus to the club's growth was the arrival of Arthur Robins in 1945 as the East Devon Professional. He took an interest in the affairs of the Town Club, tried to attract retiring soldiers into taking up the game of golf and got up a monthly competition in which he himself played.

Re-formation

At the same time the main club's Secretary, Commander Bourne, set about establishing an administrative structure, for which, he felt, there was a real need.

"I have found it most unsatisfactory having no official representative with whom I could deal regarding the Town Club matters: during the past years I have discovered there is one lady member who has been living in Exmouth for years. I have also picked up another lady playing on the course who said she was a member but had not, in fact, paid a subscription to Mr Shand, and she appeared to me to be ineligible for membership in any case."

A committee was therefore set up, consisting of three Town Club members plus one member from the committee of the parent club. An up-to-date list of members became a requirement and subscriptions – which were raised to one and a half guineas – were to be promptly paid. In return for the increase, the membership limit was raised to forty and the hours of play extended:

- Thursday and Saturday from 1 p.m. (instead of 2 p.m.).
- Every other weekday from 5 p.m. to dusk.
- Sunday: all day (instead of from 1 p.m.).

Members were not allowed to use the clubhouse but could leave their clubs at the Professional's shop "on payment of the usual charge". Names of candidates for the Town Club were to be submitted to the East Devon Committee, who had the right of refusal. These terms were approved by both committees in January 1947.

Expansion

In the early 1950s permission was given for friendly matches to be arranged with other clubs. The first to be played were against Exeter and Churston. There was an influx of "new blood" in 1951, when Exmouth Golf Club closed and membership was offered to its artisans' section, nine of whom "came over". Since they lived in Exmouth and the Town Club was established for Salterton residents it was thought fair to charge them a higher subscription, which was set at £2.5s.0d. Numbers gradually rose until in the late fifties there were 21 members from Budleigh, 11 from Exmouth and 4 green staff who had become members at the Town Club's suggestion.

Accommodation

A larger membership required better accommodation. The club had always been based at the top of Northview Road in what was called "the garages". This consisted of a long, almost circular wall with a bastion at either side of the entrance, one of which the club used as a trolley shed. In 1956 a large wooden shed was bought by the members and set up within this circle. This has recently been refurbished with four replacement windows and smart new paintwork and carpeting. In 1997, to mark the 50th anniversary of its re-establishment after the war in 1947, the club was presented by East Devon with a print of the Royal and Ancient Golf Club, and this now hangs in the clubhouse.

Club's Future in Jeopardy

In 1989 members were concerned to learn of proposals which would lead to the dissolution of the Town Club. It was agreed that every avenue should be explored, with a view to the club remaining in existence. The threat arose from the proposal by Clinton Devon Estates to sell off the land occupied by the Town Club as a building plot.

If this went through, East Devon Golf Club was prepared to offer membership to all members of the Town Club over a period of time and with some arrangement to accommodate the difference in fees. However, as planning permission was not granted for development of the site, this particular problem was quite quickly resolved.

Proposed Amalgamation

In 1994 the Management Committee of East Devon proposed that the Town Club be dissolved and its members be absorbed into the main club. The reason behind the proposal was the committee's concern over the ever increasing pressure on the course caused by the sheer volume of play that it had to sustain.

It was felt that the pressure came from members rather than visitors. At the time there were 480 full playing members of East Devon plus 40 Town Club members. If the Town Club members were absorbed gradually into the main club without raising the 'ceiling' of 480 full playing members, there would be some relief from the pressure, as there would be a reduction in the total number of members permitted to play on the course.

It was agreed that the Town Club would lose its identity but it was pointed out that this was a problem which many artisans' clubs had had to face. In Devon the artisans' clubs at Exeter, Thurlestone, Tavistock and Torquay had all closed in recent years. Budleigh Salterton Town Club was one of only three artisans' clubs remaining in the county.

Faced with the possibility of closure, it quickly became evident that the Town Club members strongly wished for it to continue. Additionally, its existence had always been encouraged and supported by the Clinton family. As a result, the East Devon "proposal" remained just that; the Town Club continued as before.

Appendix VI

PICTURE GALLERY

Gentlemen on the 1st tee, c.1903 with C.E. Pine-Coffin driving.

Another photo of gentlemen driving on the 1st tee, c.1903.

C.E. Pine-Coffin and his wife Lilian, with three caddies on the 17th green, c.1903. It is thought that the player with his back turned is Major General Henley T. Bartlett.

The Clubhouse with 'bicycle shed' removed, c.1913.

Watercolour of the links by A R Quinton, c.1920.

The Clubhouse, c.1950.

Ladies on the 11th tee, c.1960.

The 12th fairway, c.1960.

Caricature of match between Exmouth and East Devon Golf Club in 1921.

BUDLEIGH
THE MAJOR PLAYED CROQUET? FOR ENGLAND HENCE HIS STANCE
PURSEY HOLED SOME CURLY ONES
AND SO DID KENYON
R THE ALLS MALLER
WE MIGHT?
HAVE WON

The 11th and 12th holes, c.1960.

Approaching the 6th green, c.1960.